SELF-SUGGESTION

AND THE NEW HUNA THEORY OF
MESMERISM AND HYPNOSIS

BY

MAX FREEDOM LONG

AUTHOR OF

The Secret Science Behind Miracles
The Secret Science At Work
Growing Into Light

DeVORSS & CO., *Publishers*
P.O. Box 550
Marina del Rey, CA 90291

SELF-SUGGESTION
And the New Huna Theory of Mesmerism and Hypnosis.

HUNA RESEARCH ASSOCIATES was founded in 1945 by Max Freedom Long, who was its Director until 1971. Membership is open to any interested person. Research continues, but the emphasis is now on the practical application of Huna psychology in everyday life. Huna groups are active in many parts of the world. For information about Huna research, or about Max F. Long, write to:

Mrs. Dolly Ware, Curator
MAX F. LONG LIBRARY & MUSEUM
425 South Henderson
Ft. Worth, Texas 76104

INTRODUCTION

This information concerning those parts of psychology which we have come to call hypnosis, mesmerism and suggestion, is being presented as an addition to the scant literature on the ancient psychoreligious system of the Polynesians called "Huna" or the "Secret".

It is taken for granted that the reader will already have gone through the first three books dealing with the rediscovery of Huna (The Secret Science Behind Miracles, The Secret Science At Work, and Growing Into Light). But for those who come to this book without knowledge of what has been uncovered up to the present time, an appendix is supplied giving a brief outline of the ten simple elements which make possible the more practical application of certain psychological principles hitherto unknown, at least in modern days.

Although a perusal of the appendix will enable one to understand the ideas embodied in Huna, and which are frequently mentioned in this treatise, it will be well for the serious student who wishes to have all of the proofs of the verity of Huna beliefs to read the books mentioned above. In them will be found background materials which will bring one up to date on what is perhaps the most important specialized collection of anthropological findings in this century.

A word of thanks is given here for assistance in testing the theories and methods here presented for validity and practicality. Foremost amongst those to be thanked are the Huna Research Associates, and, especially, some of the more able researchers in that widely scattered organization. The secondary thanks goes to the many men who have explored the field of human consciousness in the past and who have helped bring to us such psychological knowledge as we now possess.

Max Freedom Long
Vista, California, U. S. A.

Chapter 1

Back in the dawn ages, so we are told, everything lived in the seas which covered most of the
earth. Then some of the creatures began to evolve
and to come out onto the land. Amongst these was
the serpent, and while he failed to develop legs or
wings in the many centuries which followed, he managed to develop a most amazing method of capturing
his prey.

He became the first mesmerist.

In the very new and poorly constructed semi-
science called "Psychology", so little is known as yet
of the nature of the forces of mind and thought that no
differentiation is made between mesmerism, such as
is used by the serpent, and hypnotism, in which suggestion is the key.

As all students of Huna now know, one can accumulate an extra supply of vital force very easily,
and this force, when converted to the "will" type of
energy of either the low or middle self, becomes a
strange and exceedingly potent thing.

The serpent evolved the ability to accumulate
extra vital force and to project it along the line of its
vision toward a bird. The force had a startling effect. The bird lost the power to control its actions,
and could only flutter helplessly in a state of "fasci-
nation" while the serpent wriggled near, reached out,
and began to devour it.

Close observers have noted that Mother Nature
provides an anesthetic for the prevention of pain in

3

many of her smaller creatures who must serve as food for the others. The bird or the rabbit faints and becomes unconscious just as the snake reaches it. It is popularly believed that this death is caused by fright, but the evidence of Huna indicates that, with the close approach of the mesmerist serpent, the full power of the surcharge of vital force strikes the victim and causes the unconsciousness.

Human mesmerists have demonstrated similar powers by walking into a room where volunteer subjects are seated and waiting. The mesmerist then sweeps his gaze down the row, projects his mesmeric force, and the more sensitive of the subjects tumble unconscious to the floor, lying there for several minutes before returning to consciousness. No suggestion is given. Both the serpent and the mesmerist rely on the impact as the executioner does on the shock of the electrical current.

Another point which is not well understood by the psychologist is that it is the low self (subconscious) which is affected by the vital force shock which is directed and put into such violent action by the mesmerist.

Birds and animals are all low self creatures. Only man has added to his inherited animal or low self, a middle self (a conscious mind self) which in turn has a connection with a still higher self (the Superconscious) which still is not recognized in the text books.

Over a hundred years ago, mesmerism came to public notice because of the healing work of a Dr. Anton Mesmer. He used it and it came to be named for him. His healing was spectacular as well as successful. He soon became famous through the whole of Europe.

He called the force "animal magnetism", and believed that when he was more highly charged with it than a patient, it would flow from his body to that of the patient and would bring about healing. The very fact that he expected this flow of the force, acted as a mental command to cause it to flow, and it did.

But like the serpent, he sometimes caused so much vital force to enter one who was waiting to be healed, that fluttering movements, hysteria or even unconsciousness resulted. This unconsciousness was supposed to be sleep, but it was something very different. However, it gave rise to the belief that sleep and mesmerism were in some way related.

In England, some time after Dr. Mesmer was gone, Dr. James Braid, working on this problem of mesmeric sleep, made what he considered a very remarkable discovery. He found that "suggestion" could produce the same artificial sleep. In addition he discovered that by having a patient stare in a certain way at a small bright object held well above the eye level, he could produce this form of sleep without (so he thought) the use of either suggestion or anything resembling magnetic force.

Not knowing what lay behind mesmerism, he did not realize that suggestion always contains a slight amount of vital force - Mesmer's "animal magnetism" - or that suggestion can be silently administered just by expecting the subject to fall asleep when causing him to stare at a bright eye-tiring object. (Simple tiring of the eyes causes natural sleep. Given the element of suggestion or the impact of a charge of vital force directed by the will,

5

the sleep produced is artificial.)

From Huna we learn that suggestion is the planting of a thought or idea in the mind of the subject, either by vocal or telepathic means. We further learn that an implanted idea has no mesmeric or hypnotic power at all unless mesmeric force is added to the idea at the time it is created or while it is being implanted. One may say to a friend,"Go jump in the lake", but, lacking the mesmeric force to go with this idea as it is given to the friend, he does not react to it even in the slightest way. On the other hand, if a hypnotist gave this idea in the form of a suggestion accompanied by enough mesmeric power, the subject would obediently begin to look for a lake into which to jump.

We may well marvel that men as clever as were Mesmer and Braid, should fail to unravel the mystery of what happens in mesmerism and suggestion. For one who knows Huna, it seems so very simple. But overlook it they did - and in doing so, they overlooked the most important element in the whole matter.

This MOST IMPORTANT ELEMENT is the fact that a simple idea, when filled with mesmeric force, will cause the low self of another to react in a surprising way. MOREOVER, one's own low self will react in much the same manner when given SELF-SUGGESTION.

One can give himself self-suggestion easily and quickly. It takes little training and almost no physical exertion. Once it has been given, the low self takes over and does all the work of putting the suggestion into action. This furnishes us with a tool of the greatest value. What things we fail to be able to do, no matter how we square our jaws and vow to bring about the change, can be accomplished without strain for us by the low self, once it has been given an idea heavily charged with mesmeric force.

One other point needs to be noted. This is that when a suggestion is to be given to the low self, it must have its normal charge of vital force made inactive through relaxation of the body and its controlling part of mind. In the course of this relaxation, its "will" must also be relaxed and made almost inactive, otherwise the middle self, who acts as the mesmerist-hypnotist in giving the force-charged idea as a suggestion, will not be able to implant it in the low self where it will cause the automatic reaction to begin.

Modern hypnotists have learned that slight tiring of the subject's eyes causes a weariness which will soon bring bodily relaxation. (Actual sleep is to be avoided.) This relaxed condition is needed to make the subject ready to accept suggestion, but the whirling disk with its painted spiral, now so popular, or the old bright point of light held above the eye level of the subject, have little to do with actual mesmerism or hypnosis. In the case of the factory hand who is put to sleep by the eye strain of machine parts moving constantly before him, that is sleep, not hypnosis. Nor is the beady eye of the serpent what causes the bird to become mesmerized.

A popular misconception has been that sleep suggestion, when administered by a phonograph or tape recorder is effective. There is no mesmeric force in mechanically spoken words. Such words can be only a reminder to the low self. True, if the low self is given self-suggestion or is "conditioned" by being hypnotized by an operator and commanded to accept the mechanically spoken words as true suggestion, results follow, these coming as post hypnotic reactions. Sleep recordings have been at their best as builders of memory impressions. In a state of light sleep the low self will hear and often remember things if they are repeated over and over - such as words and phrases in a foreign language.

Conversely, sleep suggestion administered by voice to a child or adult can attract the attention of the sleeper and sink into his low self. The breaking of childish habits has been easy with this method, while all but impossible by scolding or other non-suggestive use of force when the child is awake and its "will" is active and defensive.

In an article published some time ago, Howard Van Smith stated that Dr. Boris Sidis, a psychologist and professor at Harvard University, undertook to use suggestion on his sleeping son, Billy, in order to determine the value of such methods in hastening education. The learning process was not only hastened, it was made effortless in so far as remembering things was concerned. At the age of three years the child was using a typewriter. At four he was reading text books with comprehension. At seven he had finished the elementary grades of public school, taking but five months to go through all eight grades. At the age of eight, he completed, in six weeks, the entire high school course, and invented the perpetual calendar which is still much used. His ability to reason as well as remember developed with the same swiftness and he could grasp abstract ideas with ease. At the age of eleven he lectured by invitation of the Harvard dons and discussed the theory of the fourth dimension, also pointing out what he considered a defect in the Einstein theory of relativity. Unfortunately, he died in 1944 before the full possibilities of the method could be determined. His sister, Helene, was handled in a less intensive manner and did not pass her college entrance examinations until her fifteenth year.

Neither of the Sidis children had unusual mental ability if judged by the usual intelligence tests of the time, but work done with them matches rapidly accumulating evidence which shows that, given the properly charged and vitalized ideas when in a receptive condition, the low self can and will memorize and otherwise react as by magic. We who are the middle selves, and who live in the body with the low self, have a natural reasoning power, but in order to use it, we must have the proper material in the form of stored memories to work with - to recall and to compare. Given a mass of such memories by suggestion, the reasoning process will grow and the middle self learn swiftly to use the stored knowledge.

There, in a largish nut shell, we have a brief outline of mesmerism and suggestion as presented by Huna to add to and correct the little which is generally known. Let us now consider some of the details.

First, it may be well to admit the fact that few of us wish to learn to use mesmeric suggestion as professionals. Most of us will use self-suggestion.

The goal and reward of self-suggestion is the control of the low self to bring about its full cooperation in all the things, we, the middle selves, decide should be done. There are some delightful and highly valuable things which can come from such cooperation.

To begin with we can break habits which have defied us for years. The defiance always stems from the low self and not until it is caused to make the correction itself, will it be done swiftly and effortlessly.

Then there are all the good things the low self can do in matters of bettering health, stopping pain, developing better learning capacity, and providing us with a cheery mood instead of the "blues". One gets sound and restful sleep, a cessation from worry, and peace of mind. When the low self is given the right suggestion it will respond by making the tasks of the day something to be performed with pleasure and cheerfulness instead of with wearisome effort.

Compared with the usual struggle to stop smoking, and the days and nights of inner conflict which so often ends in failure, self-suggestion is a telephone conversation in which the middle self gives orders before hanging up and rushing away to the dance or theater, certain that the orders will be faithfully and fully obeyed.

At this point Huna leaves the standard text books on suggestion and takes one on and out into the realm where greater rewards begin to materialize.

The most wonderful thing of all is that full co-operation can be obtained from the low self in making contact with the High Self and inviting it to take its proper part in the three-self, or normal, way of living. This can gain us intuitive guidance and endless direct and indirect help. This is where miracles become possible.

It is rather necessary that one come to understand the mysterious and intangible things involved in any use of suggestion. To begin with we can do no better than to return to Dr. Mesmer and have a close look at what he actually succeeded in doing. It makes little difference that he was wrong in his early belief that he could draw animal magnetism (our vital force, and the "mana" of Huna) from magnets which he held in his hands or carried in his pockets, since we now know that magnetism in metals is not what is found in the human body as vital force. We must ask what it was that Mesmer used, and where it came from.

What he did is no secret. He made as strong a mental effort as he could to attract magnetism into his body from magnets. He imagined himself becoming fuller and fuller of the magnetism, until he carried a charge that was very large indeed. This worked in a strange way. When he imagined the magnetism as a living animal force, and imagined that he was becoming more and more highly charged with it, he inadvertently caused his low self to increase its supply of vital force. His low self was able to add to the normal charge in his body in an unexpected way.

Once so charged, it must be remembered, his touch allowed the vital force to enter the patients, to cause all the reactions that were later recognized as signs that hypnosis was taking effect. But the reaction to mesmerism was much greater than to later hypnosis. Patients often became violently ill, fell down in fits, or seemed to lie for a time in trance as if dead, only to recover, entirely cured.

We must not overlook what he was NOT doing. He was not consciously using suggestion, at least not the kind of suggestion known later under the heading of hypnosis. However, because he held the strong

11

intention and purpose of causing the magnetic force to leave him, enter the body of the patient, and bring about a cure, there must have been a certain amount of telepathic suggestion administered.

The mesmeric healings were made by the use of a large amount of vital force combined with a small amount of suggestion. In the later hypnotic healing efforts, almost no mesmeric force was used, but the amount of suggestion was great. The first system worked much better than the second. This was probably because a suggestion is an idea which is planted in the low self of the patient by the operator. If this idea is highly charged with the vital force under the direction of the "will" or command of the middle self, it impresses the patient's low self greatly and causes it to react in the desired manner. If the idea is barely empowered with the force, it gets only a slight response.

Dr. Mesmer became the center of a storm in medical circles. It could not be denied that he had brought about many cures, but his theory of animal magnetism could be, and was, violently attacked by his enemies. They demonstrated rather conclusively that holding a magnet in the hands did not give one the mesmeric power. Even Dr. Mesmer eventually conceded the point, but he laid stress on the fact that the force, while not of the metallic magnet type, still was a similar animal force and that it could be generated in the body.

His enemies would have none of his corrections. They were thoroughly prejudiced. However, some of Mesmer's friends continued to experiment with the force and to produce similar effects with resultant healing. Moreover, there are recorded observations of the fact that Mesmer and his followers could place their hands on various things or objects and transfer the charge of vital force to them. Tubs of water were charged in this way by Mesmer, and iron rods were placed so that one end protruded from the water of the tub. Several iron rods were placed in each large tub, and, when the patients came to the charged tubs and grasped the rods, the force which was stored in the water entered them through the rods and they reacted in the same way that other patients had done when touched directly by the famous healer.

Baron Jules Du Potet, a friend of Mesmer, carrying on this experimental transfer of the force, made a name for himself by charging certain trees. His patients came to them, touched them or had themselves bound to a tree with strong cords so that they would not fall away from it and lose contact if rendered unconscious for a time by the thing we now call "mesmeric shock". The healings were numerous.

Trees do not offer silent suggestion of the telepathic sort, or vocal suggestion. Later critics of mesmerism as a healing system make much of this, especially when they claim that all healing must come from the use of hypnotic suggestion. Not in modern texts on psychology will the answer to this puzzle be found, but in Huna. Furthermore, the answer given by Huna at this juncture needs to be written in letters a foot high to insure that it will be given full attention and that it will not be forgotten.

Huna tells us that the large charges of vital force used in mesmerism or suggestion MUST BE DIRECT - ED to cause them to act in the special ways, otherwise the charges will soon be dissipated and will fade without accomplishing a thing.

13

The directing is done by the middle self, and its "will" is the tool which it uses to give and enforce the direction. This is easily grasped and accepted, but next comes something quite incredible, even if proven true by what often happens when vital force is so directed and set to work causing effects.

The middle self "will" which is vital force impregnated in some way with an element of the conscious self, takes on a peculiar quality and shows a strange and enduring power. It seems to mix with the vital force of the body of the healer and to remain in the mixture. Note what happened when the force was placed in the tubs of water by Mesmer or in trees by Baron Du Potet. The surcharge of force stayed for a long time where it was ordered to go, and with it went the directing element of "will" so that when a patient touched the rods or the trees, the "will" caused the force to go into the body of the patient. Not only that, but, when in the body, to activate the very slight idea or suggestion of healing imparted by the healer when placing the vital force in the object for healing use.

There again we have the tiny element of suggestion made very great and very powerful because of the overweening size of the charge of vital force placed in it. But no one from the time of Mesmer to the present has ever understood that there was a definite force guided by a definite admixture of "will", placed in the water tubs of Mesmer or in the charged trees - and made to stay there separated to all intents and purposes from the healer who generated the original charge.

A thing never understood is that an idea - an immaterial thing which cannot be seen even under a microscope - is a material and actual thing capable of absorbing a large amount of vital force and that the force in turn can carry in it a directing amount of "will" energy from the middle self. Here are three "nothings", at least in so far as modern psychology is concerned. They are intangible, invisible and unidentifiable. By all test tube rules they should not exist. But they do exist, and this is well proven because we are able to observe them in action and to note the very definite results which they produce when applied as the basic forces and materials of suggestion - that is, a suggested idea plus a charge of vital force directed by the "will".

It is quite possible that these unbelievable things might not have been understood, or even guessed to exist, for a long time to come had not the ancient Huna lore been rediscovered.

In passing, it may be well to remind ourselves of the Polynesian native priests who were expert at the use of the shock charges of mesmeric force. Not only did they, like some of the medicine men of the American Indian tribes, know how to use the force to render a subject unconscious by a touch of a finger, but they made a fine art of charging throwing sticks with mesmeric force and using them in battle. The priests often stood behind the spearsmen and tossed the charged sticks over their heads to strike the body of an opposing warrier - the contact knocking him out so that he was easily overcome. It has been suggested that this practice was also known to the very old and primitive civilization of the Aboriginals in Australia. In their boomerangs they have the world's finest throwing sticks, and these, returning to the thrower after striking the victim, would have been ideal for the carrying of shock charges of mesmeric force.

There are many people who deny the possibility that suggestion exists or that there is such a thing as genuine mesmerism or hypnosis. The slogan of this school of thought has long been, "It is only the subject's imagination at work."

A recent series of tests at Duke University did much to put this negative school of thought out of the running. Rats and mice, who, we suppose, lack characteristic human imagination which might make them wish to imitate the hypnotic state and the hypnotic responses, were the subjects of experiments. They were caged so that they would have to use either of two exits to escape. An experimenter was hidden from their sight some 8 to 15 feet away, but was able to look through a small hole in a screen to see the rodents, select one, and to try to influence it to leave by whichever exit hole was determined upon.

In the May, 1957 issue of "Fate" magazine, an experimenter, Dorothy Les Tina, explained in a short article the nature of the tests and her own experience with several tame mice purchased from a pet shop. The mice were placed in a partitioned box so that when a string was pulled from a distance, one mouse at a time would be released into a larger box in which two exit holes had been cut. As each mouse was released, she concentrated her gaze on it and tried to "will" it to leave by a selected exit. At first she got little more than the results which could be attributed to chance. Then her score began to rise, and in time she was able to make scores of 10, 12, 14 and even 15 hits out of 15 tries.

16

This experiment, carried out under the direction of Dr. Gardner Murphy, was classified as a test of the power of "mind over matter" or the power of mind to move matter - "psychokinesis". Tests had already shown that some people could influence the fall of dice, supposedly with only the power of their minds. In this case the influence was supposed to exert itself on the movements of living creatures. The writer of the article was left, she said, with some unanswered questions. Apparently she could not determine whether she had established a form of rapport with the mice and was able to influence them with telepathically transmitted suggestion, or was in some way able to influence directly their muscular movements to cause the mice to walk to the selected exit hole. In any case, we can be quite certain that the mice did not realize that attempts to influence them by suggestion were being made, and, because of a fondness for the operator, used their imagination to try to pretend a response which would match the suggestion given.

We may safely say that suggestion of the mesmeric-hypnotic sort is something real and valid. It is not imagination. It produces predictable results.

With this point settled, we may go a step farther, using Huna information as our general basis, and give a fairly comprehensive definition of suggestion - a definition which has been sadly lacking or sadly defective for the past several decades.

Suggestion, of the mesmeric or hypnotic type, is composed of a central idea which has been given the power to cause an appropriate reaction on the part of the subject by charging it with more than the normal charge of vital force. With the charge of vital force there is added a directing force of "will", which is vital force slightly changed and put to use by the middle self of man. The doubly charged idea is introduced into the low self center of consciousness of the subject, after which the reaction to it may begin.

Chapter 2

In addition to the vital force used in all forms of mesmerism and suggestion, one must consider the nature of THOUGHTS.

In modern psychological circles it is postulated that thoughts are chemical actions coupled with electrical charges in some way. The brain can be stimulated by a probe which has been mildly electrified, and the patient will then recall something that had happened earlier in his life, a scene, a sound or a series of thoughts. These memories tend to take on all the semblance of reality of a dream. The electrical ingredient in the thought process is now measured by a very sensitive instrument, the electroencephalograph, which charts the electrical activities caused in the brain by thinking or even by dreaming. But still, no one has decided what a thought may be unless it is something which leaves a small imprint on certain tissues of the brain.

In Huna, things invisible and intangible are considered just as material as things which register their qualities on one of the five senses. All substance, tangible or not, is called "mea". We have no word in English to match it.

So, to the kahunas from the earliest times, THOUGHTS WERE THINGS. And, as they traveled about the world, they left this and other concepts scattered among the peoples whom they visited.

In Asia, particularly in parts of what is now

India, there may still be found very definite indications that the kahunas had passed that way. They taught that bringing the High Self into close integration or union with the low and middle selves was the true goal of living. In India, this belief gave rise to Yoga, "the Science of Union".

From Yoga the idea of the three selves passed into Hinduism, and, with the passage of time, became contaminated by other beliefs. Today in India, the basic Huna beliefs can still be recognized, but they are badly distorted. In Theosophy, which was made up largely of borrowings from Yoga and Hinduism, one may often read, "Thoughts are things".

One may read of mana, or vital force under the name of "prana", but the three selves have become "seven bodies", and vehicles and selves are mixed together so that their true identity can no longer be recognized.

Psychology has been called "the science of consciousness", but it fails dismally to recognize consciousness when it is found in the possession of the spirits of the dead, the survival of which has been well proven by the new science, Psychic Science, the outgrowth of earlier psychical research.

The dead return - and this is the point of importance to our discussion - THEY BRING BACK THEIR MEMORIES WITH THEM.

This fact has thrown all theories covering the nature of thought out of line for the psychologists and physiologists. They cannot explain it, so they prefer to ignore it. They are also forced to ignore the fact of the human "will" although it shows itself in the activities of the spirits who return.

If the modern materialistic psychologist would

"strain over the gnat" of the Huna conception of an idea charged with vital force and "will" force from the middle self, he would certainly refuse to "swallow the camel" which is now to be selected from Huna for presentation.

The kahunas not only taught that thoughts were things, but they also explained that they were made of very real substance, even if this were invisible as well as intangible. This was called "aka" or "shadowy" substance. It was to be found in the invisible "double" surrounding and interpenetrating the physical body. Each of the three selves was said to have a body of the shadowy substance, and in these they lived as spirits after death, as well as in life.

The shadowy double or "kino aka" was the mold of the body. It provided the mold into which the seed or the embryo could grow, and it expanded to match growth in size.

Science is taking slow steps in the direction of the rediscovery of the shadowy body. It has now recognized it as a "field" which surrounds the seed and guides its growth and expansion. But no scientist has yet approached the Huna concept of a thought having a similar field - a shadowy body made of the same shadowy substance, and carried as a memory, not in the physical brain, but in the shadowy body of the man. It goes without saying, that, even should a scientist accept the fact of the shadowy bodies of thoughts, he would probably reject the idea that such thought form structures were sturdy enough to survive physical death and to be preserved as memories for use by man as a spirit.

The kahunas believed that the low self has a shadowy body which replenishes its substance and from which enough material may be taken at any time to form a very small "body" to surround each thought as it is made by an action of the consciousness of the selves and by the use of the vital force. As each tiny idea in its new shadowy body is made, it is tied by a thread of the shadowy material to the thoughts which have gone ahead and to those still to come. In this way a "cluster" of thought forms is created to embody each related set of ideas.

Once a cluster of ideas is given to the low self to preserve, it becomes a memory.

The tiny threads of invisible shadowy substance which connect thought forms, also connect the whole of the individual with things once contacted. This point brings up a peculiar quality of the shadowy body substance. It is STICKY and it can STRETCH almost indefinitely.

If a person touches the hand of another person, the shadowy body substance of each may stick as if two blobs of soft taffy were pressed together and then pulled apart. In pulling apart, a long thread of the shadowy substance is drawn out and remains as an invisible attachment connecting the two people.

Everything one touches becomes attached to one by an invisible shadowy thread, much as a spider, upon touching a twig, fastens the end of a strand of web to it before spinning out more of the strand.

These shadowy strands can also be formed when a thing is touched by the sight of the eyes, and perhaps by hearing or smelling them. But the tiny threads so formed amount to little or nothing unless they are strengthened by being put to use.

If two people meet, plan experiments together in telepathic sending of mental ideas or images, and make a good contact, a cord or strand of threads connects the pair. When they are apart and ready to experiment, their low selves (who have an instinctive way of knowing how to do certain things, just as birds have of knowing how to build nests) reach out, following the connecting shadowy strands and find each other. Along the threads they cause a current of vital force to flow, and with the flow of force can be sent reproductions of the thoughts to be transmitted telepathically. The original ideas must be remembered by the transmitter, so they are not sent as messages. They are duplicated and the duplicates sent.

When a message sent by this telepathic method comes in, the low self of the receiver takes the little thought forms and places them in the center of consciousness where the middle self can sense them. When they have been properly considered, they are stored in the memory.

As far back as the days of Mesmer, the French word "rapport" was used to name the invisible, but unmistakable connection established between the mesmerist and (1) the things he charged with his vital force and "will" mixture, or (2) the subject into whom he had poured it to bring the healing reaction.

This rapport, we learn from Huna, is made possible by the connecting shadowy threads. It has been observed many times that a suggestion can be given telepathically by an operator to a distant subject. Of course, this is not within the ken of materialistic science, so the whole matter of rapport has been attacked rather than met with an honest attempt at understanding and explanation.

The vital force may be likened to an electrical

current, but it does not necessarily have to flow. It can fill a thing and remain static. But when it is guided into flowing or moving in any way by the consciousness of the low or middle self, it can flow magnificently. Unlike electricity, which gets weaker and weaker as the wire lengthens and resistance wears it out, the vital force finds in the shadowy threads a perfect conductor which offers no resistance. It can flow great distances and arrive as strong as when it started. The shadowy substance as well as the vital force is ALIVE, and both are capable of accepting guidance when it is built into them in the form of an idea tinctured with the "will".

The shadowy substance has still another strange characteristic. When rightly handled and filled with vital force, it can grow progressively solid. It can remain invisible, or it can become visible. The spirits of the dead, who have often returned to visit the living in spiritistic seances, are often expert in manipulating their low self shadowy bodies - these being taken across to the other side of life with them at the time of physical death. Solidifying structures of shadowy body substance are called "ectoplasm". They may appear as thin and hardly visible outlines of "materializing" faces or forms at seances, or they may act as molds and be filled solidly with substance and so be, to all appearance, the dead returned temporarily to life.

Visible ectoplasmic hands may be produced by spirits to move objects, or the projecting hands and arms (or simple "rods") may remain invisible and still move objects. When heavily charged with vital force (usually supplied by the living who are attending the seances) these ectoplasmic structures can use up

24

all the vital force in an instant and so exert amazing strength. In this way pianos, heavy tables, and even living human beings can be lifted.

All of which brings us back to the matter of the ideas or sets of related ideas which are created by the middle self to be used as the core of the sugges- tions which are to be given. We can better under- stand how the low self takes these ideas, as they are produced, and surrounds them with the invisible shadowy body substance drawn from its own "double". Once the idea is encased in this substance, the charge of vital force can be poured into its ectoplasmic mold and the further charge of "will" force added to it. This will cause the low self of the subject to react as to a stern command.

The mechanism is the same no matter whether a hypnotist has made ready the suggestion and implant- ed it in the subject, or whether one is using self-sug- gestion. In the latter case, the middle self, with the automatic help of the low self, makes the suggestion and then implants it in the hidden center of the low self consciousness. There it will be "out of sight and out of mind" in so far as the middle self is con- cerned, but very much to the fore for the low self, as it is already causing it to begin to react.

This, very naturally, raises the question of where the middle self lives and creates the ideas, and where the low self lives and stores them. Huna informs us that both selves have their own shadowy bodies. That of the middle self is composed of thin- ner shadowy substance than that of the low self. Dur- ing normal waking life, the two selves blend their invisible bodies, and thus the middle self, which has no physical body of its own, comes in to live as a

25

guest and guide with the low self in the physical.

It must not be forgotten that the ideas are created by the middle self by a process of reasoning based on remembered things - the memories being supplied by the low self. But after the middle self has made the ideas and charged them for use as a suggestion, these idea structures and their charges must be given to the low self to examine, classify and store as memories. Ordinarily, a set of ideas so passed down to the low self to be stored as memories, is almost instantly classified and stored where it can be found if needed. But, when a set of thought form ideas has arrived carrying a heavy charge of vital force and a proper addition of "will" force to command the low self to react in accordance with the idea, the low self is compelled either to react or to reject the donation before it can stow it away as a memory and stop paying attention to it.

Yes, the low self can reject suggestion. Often it has a set of its own unrationalized beliefs which holds ideas quite contrary to what the command in the suggestion idea offers. Thereupon, the low self decides for itself that its own idea is better, and refuses to react to the new idea. Now and then a spirit of a dead person comes back and moves in with the low self, fully or intermittently, or it edges in at times just enough to impose its ideas on the low self. This condition falls under the heading of Abnormal Psychology and is popularly mentioned as "obsession" or multiple personality.

If there is this spirit influence behind the scenes with the low self it may be responsible for the rejection of the suggestion just as is the presence of a complexed belief.

26

What is called a "posthypnotic suggestion" by the hypnotist is one in which the low self is given a built-in time schedule for reaction in the set of ideas implanted into it. The low self reasons imperfectly, but it has a good understanding of the measurement of time and distance. When the suggestion is given that an action will be performed at a given future time, it will remain aware of the passage of time and will react on schedule.

The question of whether or not the low self can recall events and even words spoken in its presence at the time of birth has very little light thrown upon it by Huna. The Dianetics theory of L. Ron Hubbard advances the idea that one is influenced in later life by unconsciously remembered events or spoken words, these exerting undiminished compulsive power from the moment of birth onward through life. Such obstructing sets of ideas have been given the name of "engrams", and the devotees of Dianetics often spend much time trying to recall such memories in order to render them harmless.

Not content with starting at birth to turn up harmful and coercive command-memories, the "pre-clear" is often urged in Dianetics to pick up memories of similar things all the way back to conception......
then, all the way back through former incarnations.

While Huna advocates the belief that one usually has several incarnations, these occur under circumstances quite unlike those accepted by the standard Reincarnationists, little light being thrown on bringing over memories of these experiences. No mechanism is indicated or named which would make one think that memories made into shadowy body substance units are carried over from a past incarnation

27

at the times of rebirth.

The Theosophists, who follow the lines of belief laid down by the founders and by some of the later leaders, accept many things gleaned from the beliefs of the people of India, especially from Vedanta, Yoga and Brahmanism. One of the accepted beliefs is that memories of past incarnations may be recovered, and, to explain how this is possible, recourse is had to a theory that all events and all thoughts are impressed on what might be called the shadowy body of the earth - the "akasa". To recall events in a past incarnation, one has but to learn to read or recall certain memories preserved in the "akasic records". The success of making such readings, as reported by people over a period of years, has not been too impressive. Too many have remembered an incarnation as Napoleon or Cleopatra, and, sad to relate, the memories have not matched.

In the years 1956-57, few literate Americans failed to hear about "Bridey Murphy". Dr. Morey Bernstein hypnotized a housewife and regressed her to past lives. She relived in detail a former life in Ireland as Bridey Murphy. What she said during the periods of hypnotic trance and regression made a book, and an investigator was dispatched by the publisher to Ireland to see if evidence could be found to substantiate the material.

A report was made in which the investigator presented a number of his conclusions and told why he had reached them - mainly tending to show that the conditions described in the hypnotic state had really existed. The press discussed the pros and cons. Church authorities were interviewed, and some of them bitterly attacked the belief in reincarnation as well as the validity of the Bridey Murphy findings.

Later, a wordy battle was waged through the pages of magazines, some writers trying to prove that the housewife had recalled, under hypnosis, only things told her about Irish life of past years by a certain acquaintance whose name was, actually, Bridey Murphy. The implication was that there had been black fraud. There were rebuttals, and then silence. No authority existed to render a decision one way or the other.

But the interest in hypnosis and possible regression which had been aroused became general. Many amateur and professional hypnotists tried their hands at it, and some subjects came up with variations on the standard pattern of reaction. In Boulder, Colorado, Robert W. Huffman, amateur hypnotist, and his collaborating subject, Irene Specht, were responsible for the widest variation. Adding explanations to trance statements recorded on tapes, they also produced a book. It was titled, "Many Wonderful Things", and it told how Mrs. Specht, under hypnosis, was regressed to a time between incarnations when her spirit was in a "Place of rest". In the suggestions used to regress her to this point, the word "love" was much used as a part of the trance producing formula. Whether or not this caused the low self of Mrs. Specht to fasten upon the theme of "love" or not is open to question. In any event, while in hypnotic trance she described a condition in which her spirit was resting between lives and was able to see the greater verities behind living. The spirit called herself the "I am I" during trances, and preached a doctrine of love with which she sought to solve many

29

problems which were laid before her. She took up passages from the Bible and assigned new meanings to them - and once more there developed controversy and antagonism. But for some reason or other the newspapers gave this experiment scant notice.

What we do not understand, we fight and fear. This is true the world around and it has been that way in all ages. Not understanding the nature of suggestion or what makes it work, the public has come to distrust it. Some religious organizations have condemned the use of hypnosis, and the Theosophists have been issuing warnings against its use for many years, although the founders advocated the use of mesmerism for healing purposes and proudly told of how their Colonel Olcott had healed fifty cases of paralysis in Ceylon by the use of that beneficial power. Even the astute founder, Madame Helena Blavatsky, failed to recognize the fact that mesmerism and hypnosis differ only in the matter of how much or how little suggestion is mixed with how much or how little vital force and "will" force.

Later Theosophists have usually preferred to take no chances. Accepting the authority of the dictionaries rather than that of the founders, they have chosen to consider mesmerism and hypnotism one and the same thing.

The main argument against hypnosis was, and continues to be, that if one is once "dominated" by the will of another, the domination continues to a large degree, and, worst of all, the rapport which is established between operator and subject is a bond which cannot be broken. It ties, it is explained, the dominated one to the operator for life, and continues to tie him for, perhaps, all following incarnations.

30

The ability to control a subject for evil purposes, over miles of distance and years of time, is exaggerated and viewed with great alarm. The horrible example of a black school of Yoga practitioners, who misuse hypnotic power is often pointed out.

Little evidence of this master-slave relationship between operator and subject has ever been produced, but the lack of understanding of what really happens in the use of suggestion has fertilized the ground of fear.

With the increase in the numbers of amateur hypnotists in recent years, cries of alarm and indignation began to arise on every side. The consensus of opinion seemed to be, "They shouldn't be allowed to tamper with the human mind!" In response, the state legislatures set to work to make laws forbidding the use of hypnotism-mesmerism to all who are not trained to stringently high standards in the dental or healing professions.

Fortunately, no laws are being passed to encroach on personal liberty and to prevent the use of suggestion by oneself on oneself.

Self-suggestion is safe to use even if all the horrendous dangers of hypnotism, pointed out by such Theosophical writers as William Q. Judge and Dr. G. de Purucker, had been proven to be valid even to a small degree.

Dr. de Purucker, as quoted in a recent book of gathered Theosophical writings titled, "Hypnotism-Mesmerism and Reincarnation", (see page 76) says, "Autosuggestion, which means suggestion practiced upon yourself, is always right, and we should practice it continually, if it means merely suggesting to oneself night and day and all the time pictures of spiritual and moral and intellectual strength, self-control, and improvement - things of beauty, of glory, of holiness, of purity, of charity, of kindness; in short, all the great and noble virtues. Autosuggestion in this sense is right because it is simply teaching ourselves....." (It will be noted that nothing is said here of the use of autosuggestion to help heal ourselves. Some of the writers represented in this book lean to the belief that healing may prevent suffering and so the paying off of bad karma, but if this archaic belief were to be followed to the logical extreme, all forward looking Theosophists would at once set about torturing themselves.)

To sum up, we may conclude that suggestion made by a moral operator and containing only beneficial and good ideas, cannot be harmful. If the rapport between operator and subject should by chance remain unbroken for many incarnations, then, by the same argument it would have to be admitted that each of us builds thousands of strands of shadowy substance connecting us with others in a definite form of rapport. If this is so, it is unavoidable, and we will not go too far wrong in adding one more strand to a good hypno-therapist.

In self-suggestion, there can be no danger of domination by anyone other than oneself.

Chapter 3

Mesmerism may be said to be as old as the serpent, and hypnotism as old as Dr. Braid, for he coin-
ed the name for it.

Self-suggestion - called also autosuggestion and
autoconditioning - had an obscure beginning in France
around the time of World War 1. Experimenters had
been playing with the mechanism long before that,
but the first real attempt to describe the process and
the results to be obtained through its use came at
this period.

Dr. Freud, of Vienna, had already partly iden-
tified the low self of Huna under the name of the "id"
and had discovered the "complex".

Then came the first real advance. Dr. Frederick
Pierce, a professor in one of the leading New England
universities, and a psychologist, chanced to be vaca-
tioning in Switzerland. While bowling, he made the
discovery that when attention was withdrawn from
his hand and the ball it held during a period when his
attention was attracted to something other than the
game, the strength left the hand and it relaxed. With
the attention again turned to the hand, the strength
and muscular tenseness returned. This set him to
thinking. He had been puzzling over the obscurities
and empty spots in the writings of a French experimenter, and had come to realize that self-suggestion
was difficult to administer to the inner and hidden
self. He guessed that in a state of physical relaxa-

tion (this substituting for the "sleep" suggested to a relaxed patient in hypnosis) the suggestion might be administered much better.

There followed a series of experiments which resulted in the invention of a special relaxation method. He named it "Decubitus", and when back at the university, began teaching some of his pupils to use the relaxation method as a part of self-suggestion. He found that about nine out of ten of the students learned the method easily, and that all were much benefited. Soon he set to work writing a book about it.

Dr. Pierce called his book, "Mobilizing the Mid-Brain", for he accepted the theory of the day which dictated the belief that all consciousness must be resident in the brain tissues. It was published and attracted much attention in psychological circles before it was eventually allowed to go out of print - and was more or less forgotten in the fury of the battles which were developing between the several schools of psychological thought. Behaviorists did battle with Freudians. Dr. Emile Coué rose into the limelight and faded out of it with his version of self-suggestion and his formula, "Every day in every way, I am growing better and better." True, everyone tried the formula and hoped to get results similar to those produced by Dr. Coué. But they had not been taught how to construct a powerful suggestion or to relax physically in order to administer it. Psychology drifted into the doldrums and remained there.

Meantime, at Duke University, Dr. J. B. Rhine was waging a war of his own on Materialism. Basing his work on the mathematics of chance happenings, he enlisted his students in the work of experimenting with extrasensory perception. "E. S. P." became a

34

byword in many circles, and his books, while limited in their coverage of a subject already more fully explored in Psychical Research, carried the weight of the use of an accepted research method. He convinced many open-minded people that there was such a thing as telepathy, also that clairvoyance was a fact and that it could be demonstrated. His demonstrations of the power of "mind over matter", (or psychokinesis - "P. K.") were hard to ignore. The Materialists gradually learned to handle him with care. He wrote books, and he had the expectant ear of the public. Duke University became a monument to the open and inquiring mind.

To this university came Dr. Hornell Hart, and it was he who was destined to revive public interest in self-suggestion after a period of dormancy lasting over two decades.

Dr. Hart, surprisingly enough, was not a member of the faculty in the department of psychology. He headed the department of sociology, and it may be that his main interest was, at least at first, in finding some way to help students to fit more smoothly into the social structure of the class room and of the life flowing around the university outside its gates. The students were of both sexes, the men often married, with families to support, while some were fresh from military service. Many found it very hard to fit into the new circumstances in which they found themselves.

The daily change in moods of the students was great. Some days they were happy and cheerful. On other days they might be deeply sunk in a mood of discouragement, fear, resentment or anger. Often they had the "blues" for no ascertainable reason.

Dr. Hart set about finding a remedy in autoconditioning for this painful up-and-down changing of moods from day to day. He asked the help of his students to work out a remedy, taught them the few simple things they needed to know, and set them to testing out autoconditioning.

He had the students keep and chart records of their ups-and-downs in the matter of moods. The moods were roughly classified from the blackest up to the lightest, most pleasant and most helpful. The "Mood-Meter" was developed, consisting of a chart of moods and a method of recording changes in mood, both when using autoconditioning and when failing to do so.

The success of this series of experiments was so marked that there could be no question of the validity of the results or of the outstanding benefits gained. It was found that almost all of the students could learn to autocondition quickly and with little trouble. This fact made almost every reader of Dr. Hart's book, "Autoconditioning", wish to use the method and share its benefits. These were surprisingly great considering how little time or effort needed to be expended.

By the summer of 1957, Dr. Hart was in demand as a lecturer and teacher, traveling as far as Los Angeles to teach his method and explain its value. His main effort may have been to convince his audiences that autoconditioning is so beneficial that it should be learned by almost everyone, and that it is easy to learn as well as perfectly safe.

The theory which he advances in his writings is based on a belief in the "id" or subconscious as propounded by the late Dr. Freud and as accepted by all psychiatrists who hope to get employment in our government hospitals.

The middle self of Huna - popularly known as the conscious mind - he often calls the "real self" while the low self or subconscious he calls the "id", the "inner receptive mind" or the "unconscious mind".

Dr. Hart describes autoconditioning as a form of post-hypnotic suggestion in which the individual, standing as the real self, gives the suggestions to the inner receptive self. There is no recognition of the fact that these two selves are separate individuals. Hypnosis has the basic meaning of "sleep causing", and it is pointed out that while the general mechanisms of hypnosis are used to some extent, sleep is not at all a part of autoconditioning. If one goes to sleep, he warns, no results are obtained.

No attempt is made to present a theory to explain hypnosis. It is presented as something we now have come to accept as explored in full and proven out in so far as the suggestive phenomena are concerned, even if what lies behind them, hidden in consciousness, remains a mystery, a tangle, or a starting point for controversy.

With interest in autosuggestion and hypnosis beginning to grow as early as the year 1948, there had been offered several correspondence courses, some of them of the inexpensive "catch penny" kind, and a few laid out most eleborately, often with the coining of a new vocabulary of psychological terms. Some one of the several popular theories purporting to explain suggestion was usually given with arguments to support it.

Where interest is found awakening in a special field, there are usually those who appear to offer a

37

new theory purporting to explain everything, and, as in the case of the book, "Many Wonderful Things", which gave its variation on hypnotic regression into past lives, a book by Dr. Rolf Alexander came into the self-suggestion field in 1954.

His book is titled, "Creative Realism", and in it he goes well beyond the boundaries of ordinary suggestion, venturing into the realms of metaphysics at times.

He considers autosuggestion to be a form of suggestion which we can give to the subconscious while fully awake and not in even the lightest state of hypnotic trance. Autohypnosis, on the other hand, he describes as the giving of suggestion to the subconscious when it is in a state of trance, be it ever so light, or even very deep. He adds the information that one can often learn to use autohypnosis more easily if one first allows a hypnotist to administer hypnosis, throw one into a state of trance, and give one post-hypnotic suggestion to the effect that, at any later time, one need only speak a "trigger word" of command to cause one's subconscious to bring about the state of trance needed to make it receptive to new suggestion.

Going still farther, Dr. Alexander offers the theory that we are all hypnotized to a considerable degree by what has happened to or around us in our lives. He seems to blame many of our personality troubles on this form of hypnosis-without-a-hypnotist, and he offers a method which he calls "self-realization" to be used to dehypnotize ourselves. The use of this method is urged as a preliminary to the administering of autosuggestion. It is also to be used as an antidote to remaining in a suggestible trance to some extent after the use of autohypnosis.

Mention must be made of another writer of this general period when autosuggestion was once more attracting interest. Alfred Korzybski, in his book, "Science and Sanity", wrote at length about what false meanings attached to words can do to throw individuals off the line of normal mental and emotional balance. He pointed to many instances in which a misunderstanding of the true meaning of a word has caused an emotional disturbance. Reasoning, being based on a correctly understood set of word meanings in many instances, has been found to be faulty, and faulty reasoning can bring on emotional troubles to match. His reasoning is sound and his thinking has colored much in the realms of psychological conjecture, but he has added little to our knowledge of the theory or mechanics of suggestion itself.

One of the latest books to enter the general field, is "Hypnotism Handbook", by Cooke and Van Vogt. It is a careful digest of the standard methods used in administering hypnosis in professional circles. In it the authors discuss the several schools of psychological thought and their theories, but state candidly that as yet we do not know what hypnosis actually is. However, they are quick to add that we can classify rather well the things which suggestion can bring about, and know enough of the practical application of the mysterious mind force to use it very well.

They question the theory that all is "conditioning" (forming new reaction habits by repetition). They call attention to what follows when a hypnotized subject is commanded to be alert and normal in every way except that he will remain open to suggestion. The subject, under such circumstances, appears to think, reason, perform his usual work, and in every way to give evidence of being in a normal condition, except that he responds instantly to the orders of the hypnotist. It must be agreed that the theory of conditioning would have to be stretched to the breaking point to account for this type of reaction.

While "Hypnotism Handbook" is intended for the use of professionals, it can be read with profit by anyone wishing to know what the generally accepted ideas are concerning self-suggestion, and what methods are proposed for the use of the professional hypnotist desiring to help a subject learn to activate in himself suggestions given beforehand by the therapist.

The authors appear to have little enthusiasm for the use of self-suggestion when the professional is not first consulted and allowed to earn his fee. They admit that while there are methods which can be used to learn the use of autohypnosis without the help of a hypnotist, these methods "require prolonged training". Yoga practices are mentioned as examples of one long and difficult method of learning to use the art. This conclusion is sharply contradicted by the statements of Dr. Pierce and Dr. Hart, both of whom found that their students learned to use self-suggestion with ease in a matter of a few days, becoming almost expert inside a period of a month or two.

In concluding this short summary of conditions surrounding self-suggestion, it may be said that the system is so simple that all of the methods of use which have been advocated outside of professional circles are effective and practical. It is in understanding what one is doing and why, that a lack may be felt. Almost anyone can learn to write his name by patient practice, but if he can first learn to recognize the letters and learn the sounds for which they stand, the setting down of the signature will have vastly more meaning and significance.

Coming to know Huna, is like coming to know the alphabet of psychology and learning to read the sounds of the letters. We do anything better after we have learned why each step is to be taken.

Chapter 4

Using self-suggestion is a simple process which may be divided into three steps: First, quite naturally, one must decide what is to be suggested to the low self by the middle self - to the subconscious by the conscious mind self. Second, one relaxes the body, stills the trains of thought that may be running through the mind, and, when the low self is in this way made ready to accept suggestion, the third step is taken. This third step is to give the suggestion to the low self either aloud or silently.

One may succeed in getting some response from the low self on the very first attempt to use self-suggestion, but usually it takes a little period of practice before one gets a full and swift response.

Now let us elaborate and detail the steps. It is best to begin with something very simple and easy. If the ultimate goal is a hard one like breaking a habit such as that of smoking or overeating, it is best to wait until the low self has been taught by easy stages to accept suggestion on lesser things, and has become accustomed to react properly to bring about little changes. One learns to crawl, then to walk, and then to run. An attempt to reverse the process and start with the running cannot help but be a waste of time.

A bit of theory needs to be considered at this point. All who have learned to use suggestion agree upon this: YOU as the middle self, must have faith that what you suggest is possible and good and desirable. YOU must clear your mind of doubt, otherwise you pass on the doubts to the low self, and prevent it from believing what you tell it is going to take place.

It is difficult at first for the middle self to believe that what it suggests to the low self will be brought about by it with swift and effortless work behind the scenes. Going slowly and learning that the low self is responding, even if very slightly, will make all the difference. "Nothing succeeds like success" is an old saw which applies here to perfection. Nothing builds confidence in the middle self as does the discovery that the low self is actually responding.

A simple little test of self-suggestion is one having to do with the yawn. For some reason, as we all know, a yawn is something that carries an almost ludicrous suggestive power. The low self seems almost unable to resist it. Let one person in a room begin to yawn, and soon others will begin to feel an almost uncontrollable desire to yawn.

Make this test on your low self. It is self-suggestion in its simplest form. Try it and see if you are one of the ninety out of a hundred who can give this suggestion effectively on the first attempt.

Get off by yourself where you will not be disturbed for a short time. Sit down and make yourself very comfortable. Run your attention over your legs, arms, hands and wherever you find the muscles are not relaxed, making them relax their tension. The face and jaw muscles and those of the hands are the ones most apt to be slightly tense, and the mind will always have to be slowed down and its thought trains stopped so that there is a relaxation of thinking activities or mental tensions. It may take several

43

minutes, and on this first attempt to relax it is well to do a good job because you will be setting a pattern of sorts for your low self to follow in subsequent periods of relaxation.

When you come to feel relaxed and resting in body and mind, begin slowly and without effort to make a mental picture of yawning. There is a great difference between the ways people make mental pictures of a yawn. No two will do it exactly the same way, but that makes little difference as long as the basic idea of a yawn is brought into the focus of consciousness.

You may picture others yawning, or yourself, or you may talk about yawning in words - silently or aloud - talking to yourself. Keep dwelling on the idea of yawning, imagining yourself yawning and enjoying it. Your low self may respond almost the moment you begin to think of a yawn, or it may take time - up to several minutes - but soon it will accept the idea and the mental picture which you are holding with the intention that the low self will accept it as its own and react to it. When it does accept the idea, it will cause the yawn. It may cause a whole series of yawns, and if so, be sure you enjoy them, lest you outline another response pattern that is not good. Always tell yourself (and the low self will hear you) that the thing suggested is good and pleasant. Then be sure that you take time to enjoy whatever it is after the low self suddenly brings it about. This holds true in everything, even in enjoying fresh courage after self-suggesting it and having it replace fear of failure in some situation, or even after suggestion has caused the low self to stop a nagging pain or a bothersome worry cycle which is keeping you awake at night. The low self loves praise. Be quick to say, "Fine! Good job! Well done!"

The low self is another "self", according to Huna. Believe this or not, as you please, but address it as you would a close friend with whom you live in the body, and who can do things with the body and with your feelings and energy which you cannot do. Call it "You" and give it quiet orders if you wish. Or, if you have learned to talk to your low self through the use of the pendulum, and have learned by what name your low self likes to be called, use that name.

The two selves are so closely associated in the body that one may also say "We" if the middle self is planning to do its very best to help bring about conditions which are to be desired, such as conditions in which one begins to make more friends. In such a case one might say, "We are going to begin tomorrow to do the things which will make friends for us. We will be cheerful and friendly and will take a genuine interest in those we meet. We will be TRULY interested in them and the things they do, say, think and desire. We will do what we can to help them, and soon we will have friends all around us who will love and help us in turn."

If you make up your mind very firmly to work to accomplish something, half the job is done. The other half is to get the low self to believe that you are firm in your determination and to share it with you. Just making the decision as a middle self, with the low self only notified of what you have decided to do will get you little help from it. In fact, it may trip you up before you go far. To make the low self share your determination and do its very important part to bring about the new condition, you must take

45

time to relax the low self in the body, make it ready to accept the suggestion, and then give the suggestion. You may repeat the giving of the suggestion a number of times before you get the full cooperation of the low self, but in time it will begin to pull its share of the load.

There are two ways in which the low self reacts. One way is to start, upon being given a command with suggestion, to do something it already knows how to do, such as control a bodily process or imitate a way of doing things which it has observed, or to do things which it knows well how to do, but which it does not like to do. This first way is true "conditioning". The second makes use of things already known, simply causing them to be put into action, as does the hypnotic command to a subject to act like a dog. The subject does not have to learn to act like a dog. He already knows enough about dogs to be able to imitate barks, growls and waggings. Conditioning begins at the very beginning.

When you teach a dog to do a trick by making him do it over and over until he is expert at it and obeys your order immediately, you have "conditioned" him or taught him a new set of chain reactions in which thoughts and muscular movements follow one after the other. We can train the low self to perform tricks in exactly the same way.

Learning to use a typewriter, or to write, or spell or skate, come under the heading of conditioning. Almost every word you write on the typewriter or with a pen is a trick in itself. Like the command to the dog to "sit up", we learn a whole series of commands or things which stimulate the conditioned response. One sits down at the typewriter and thinks of a word or of a single phrase. This thinking is all the command the trained or conditioned low self needs. It types the word or phrase. It also spells the word. You, the middle self do little more than stand by to decide what triggering command thoughts are to be decided upon and given to the low self. The team work between the two selves is a thing wonderful to contemplate. But we must not forget that we had, in the beginning, to teach the low self day after day to respond to the thought or sound of a word and to learn to spell it. We must remember the first slow words and lines on the typewriter before the low self learned or was conditioned to that skill.

The amusing test with the yawning may be carried on further and into the realm of a conditioned reflex (as such things are often called). All that is needed is to teach the low self to respond to the command, "Yawn". Once it learns to respond after a series of relaxation and suggestion sessions, you need only give the command, "Yawn", and in short order the low self will respond by making the whole man have an irresistible desire to yawn, and by following up with the yawn itself. You can even teach the low self to respond with a yawn to a command given in some other way. The sound of a bell could be used, or some other word. It is all a matter of training.

It is all but impossible to tell exactly where triggering off a conditioned reaction chain ends and where the use of suggestion to set the low self into motion begins. One seems to run into the other. That is why it is best to repeat suggestions. The low self will have its response quickened each time we recall the idea given in the suggestion the day before and present it anew. Each time the idea is recalled and recharged with "will" and vital force, then given back to the low self, the fresh charge stimulates proper and continuing action.

On the other hand, the repetition, once reactions start to come along regularly, acts to condition or train the low self and provide it with a habit of doing certain things in certain ways, also doing them more and more skillfully as the reaction is learned and becomes more and more automatic.

The low self is a creature of habit. Once it has learned to do a thing in a certain way, it uses the same ideas each time as a pattern by which to work. When a new pattern is given to it, considerable pressure of the suggestive order must be exerted day after day until the low self is made to stop trying to use the old pattern and accept the new.

Trying with only the middle self "will" to force the low self to give up an old pattern or reaction, while accepting for use a new and different pattern, leads to Churchillian "Blood, sweat and tears" in many cases, especially where we find narcotics, tobacco or alcohol being used habitually. Suggestion, which adds massive ingredients of vital force to the new pattern ideas, makes the "will" a hundred times more effective by giving it a tool with which to work. The "will" may be likened to a man trying to pull a nail with his fingers. The charge of vital force may be likened to a claw hammer, and with the hammer, the nail comes out of the wood with ease.

Chapter 5

The making of the idea to be used in self-suggestion is a simple matter if the idea is to be simple and familiar. One finds no difficulty in recalling all memories of yawns which may be needed to work over and draw upon so that a fresh mental image of a yawn can be constructed. Nor does one have to put more than a small amount of vital force and "will" into the idea before it is called to the attention of the low self and begins to act as a suggestion.

But when it comes to making a general idea which may include several steps or stages to complete an action or to bring about a new condition in the body or surroundings, the low self cannot help much. It can give all the memories needed by the middle self to work with, but it does not say gleefully, "Hey! that's something I know all about! So you want me to yawn? Stand back and give me time. I'll yawn for you, and how!"

If one plans to construct a set of idea images which will be used to suggest something new to the low self, or something which will force it to change a fixed habit it has already developed, the low self may look on silently and with apprehension. In some cases it may be frightened and very doubtful, or it may be rebellious and headstrong, already deciding that it will resist.

It is the better part of valor to be cautious in

making one's approach under these conditions. The middle self will do well to walk carefully around and around the proposition, viewing it from all angles before getting down to work on it.

One of the easier approaches, and one which brings delightful results with very little effort, is to be found in setting the mood for next day. We all tend to fall into the habit of carrying certain moods around with us day after day. If something happens to change the mood to a lower or darker level of "blues" or discouragement or fear, then we live at that level for a time. Or if an event is such that it makes us excited, happy, eager or confident, we rise to that level for a time, enjoying it to the full, and then, as the old habit pattern brings pressure to bear on the low self, we sink back to the usual level.

Dr. Hart's method of raising and keeping the mood level has been discussed. In Dianetics and Scientology a similar effort was made and the mood level was charted as "tone". Tone levels were numbered from low to high and the things which caused low tone were listed in contrast with the things which caused high tone. The high tone levels were pointed out to be identifiable by comparison to one's views on life and one's daily actions. The goal and criterion were normal living. Normal living included among other things the acceptance of responsibility such as is found in marrying, earning a living and serving the general social structure of the community by having children and rearing them well. Other and less difficult things were also listed as normal, and the individual was urged to get rid of his "engrams" as fast as possible so that a rise in tone could be more rapidly accomplished.

50

It all boils down in the last analysis to something which must be taken up and considered before the mood level is attacked. This is the matter of getting oneself to WANT to make a change for the better. Odd as it may seem, a very considerable number of people are found who are so complexed or so influenced by obsessing spirits that they do not wish to be happier - to have the happiness that comes with the brighter moods. For these individuals and the ones who are psychotically deranged and who live in a mood of unreasonable excitement and continuous exhilaration, neglecting the duties of life, self-suggestion is not the answer. They need a psychiatrist. If the mood into which they sink becomes too low and dark, there is grave danger of a stay in a mental hospital.

There is the benefit of better health and energy to be had by using self-suggestion, and if one finds in oneself no interest in feeling active, alert and physically and mentally fit, that also is a danger sign. What we have come to call "psychosomatic illness" comes from bad mental conditions, and many who are ill fall under the classification of those who "enjoy illness". These also need mental therapy from a doctor rather than urging to try to get past their heavy complexes or obsessions and on with the use of self-suggestion.

The majority of us, however, are near enough to being normal, even if subject to mood and other changes. Self-suggestion is for us if we can overcome the habit of living each day with changes of any kind resisted by the low self, and can sit down and take stock of our lives, ourselves, our reactions to those around us and our attitude toward the work we

51

have to do.

There are many things which cannot be scored on a mood chart, but which can be recognized in ourselves if we ask, "What, if anything, is bothering me? What do I dislike? Why do I dislike it? What do I find too hard or too tiresome or too boring?"

When we have written down the answers which come to us concerning the things we do not like, we can ask, "What do I want? How would I like to change myself? How would I like to have people treat me? Would I like to be more loved, recognized, praised or admired?"

Out of such little examinations, especially if one tries to write down the answers, there will come all sorts of unexpected ideas. Many of these will be provided by the low self if it is invited from the first to give its feeling in the matter of likes and dislikes. Betimes one may do well just to sit quietly with pencil in hand and wait for the low self to get its ideas across. It is a new process to the low self and it may take a little time to get the knack of it, but given time, it will begin to present ideas as if they were old memories suddenly floating into the mind.

These old memories are very often the recalls of things which came earlier in one's life and which, at the time, caused one to be much moved and to come to great determinations to do or not to do, to try or not to try, something. Old lost and forgotten ambitions, plans and desires will gradually be called to your attention by the low self, and as they are brought up out of the memory they should be studied carefully and one should make a firm decision as to whether the old things once desired are still desirable or have served their purpose and should be given

52

up with finality. Old fears, angers, resentments and other things which were accompanied by strong emotional reactions in the past need especial study and rationalization. To reason about them and their meaning as they may apply today is to rationalize the impressions and clean them up before letting them sink back again into the memory storage.

A host of our small feelings of fretfulness, dissatisfaction, dislike and, especially, restlessness have their roots in old things such as these under discussion. If left unrationalized in terms of what they actually mean today - not what they meant in days past - they can trip us up as if they were tiny complexes. Take time to clean house mentally with this catharsis and prophylaxis, then you will have the board swept clear before you as you lay out your plans to decide what betterment in moods you will most enjoy and will begin working to get.

In the experimental work done by the Huna Research Associates, a simple assignment was given to find out approximately how long the average Associate could hold his attention on a selected mental image before tiring and having the mind let go its grip. This assignment was decided upon because of the disagreement on many points by authors of books on concentration and meditation. Some writers stated one thing, some another.

Among the oldest of the writings to be consulted were those of Patanjali, whose "Yoga Aphorisms" have been a favorite text in Yoga circles since about 140 B. C. This early psychologist, as well as one of the several Kapilas who wrote on Yoga at an even earlier date, may have had some contact with Huna. Both wrote in Sanskrit, which is not a very flexible language and which is not well adapted to hiding double meanings in words (as was the language used by the ancient men who evolved Huna). But symbol words such as were used in Huna are still to be recognized in the Sanskrit texts. All of the aphorisms were originally called "sutras", which gives the odd meaning of "threads", and commentators have been quick to explain that this has something to do with the act of sewing or uniting things, being a reference to the basic goal of Yoga - that of uniting the lower self with the higher. This fits neatly into the Huna theory that the two lower selves are connected by a large thread or cord of shadowy body substance to the High Self. These cords may not be used for the normal interchange of vital force and thought forms when the low self is prevented from doing its part in the interchange by a feeling of guilt or by a complex of one kind or another. Another symbol found in Huna and often in the Huna parts of the Bible, as well as in the religious writings of India, is that of the "path" and of its being blocked or open. In early Yoga texts the "gunas", or "knots", are often mentioned, and one may assume with safety that the original Huna meanings of the symbolic thread and knot were well known, even if lost in a maze of speculation in the later periods.

Patanjali wasted little time on the many and complicated bodily postures and breathing exercises which came later to be regarded as so necessary for the gaining of proper mental control and concentration. He advised the beginner to make himself comfortable in a seated position, then to get on with the business of quieting the mind and stopping the trains of thought flowing through it in haphazard manner.

In passing, it is interesting to note that in Yoga circles their concentration and meditation exercises were aimed at three major benefits. First there was "Hatha" yoga, or the department in which physical good was the goal. Next there came "Raja" yoga or the work to correct and perfect the reasoning and "will" power of the middle self and to bring the low self under control. Third came the goal which over-shadowed all else - that of making and keeping normal contact with the High Self - the attainment of "union".

These are also the goals of Huna, and in self-suggestion we begin with the first two steps, leaving the third to come later.

To get back to the matter of tests made by the Huna Research Associates. Tests were carried on to see how long a mental image could be held. It was quickly learned that the low self is in control of all efforts to keep a given image in the focus of attention. It tires quickly, and despite the determination of the middle self to keep the attention on the image, will allow it to slip back into the memory storage. If the middle self is not alert, the low self will substitute some other image and start a train of thought more to its liking.

Some Associates reported a holding time for images of hardly more than five seconds. Others, especially those who had taken training in concentration, reported holding times of up to three minutes. The average was about thirty seconds.

More experiments were tried, and in these the mental picture was allowed to move. Faces smiled, and heads nodded, lips moved and spoke, eyes opened and closed. With this changing of the image, the tiring or exhaustion of vital force on the part of the low self appeared to be avoided. It was as though the two selves were able to use up the force in one idea or mental image, then lay it aside and take up another, much as one might exhaust the charges in one tiny storage battery after another. The ideas in their molds of shadowy body stuff, after being allowed to sink back into the memory storage place for an instant to absorb more vital force, could be recalled and held again for the same length of time. Moving trains of these images could be held with ease because they moved on as fast as the force in them was used up. But, although the time of concentration was extended almost indefinitely, the focus was diffused instead of pointed and sharp.

The experiments helped evolve a method of concentration in which the image concentrated upon was let go as if to rest it for an instant, then called back and held again. This gives a feeling of rhythmic and slow "pulsing" of the image. It allows an image to be held for a long period of time, and this is very useful. It allows the mental image to be built up more strongly and made to hold a larger and larger charge of "will" force. The pulsing method also prevents the intrusion of other images or the marching across the stage of mind of a parade of unrelated ideas. It may be said to mark a milestone of discovery in the preparation of ideas to be used in self-suggestion.

Other ways of making mental images were tested, such as compounding sets of little ideas which were needed to make up a larger general concept composed of a whole cluster of thought forms. Here the minds of some were found to be able to grasp and hold more than the minds of others - hold wider and more detailed pictures or images. For instance, in building a picture of oneself going out to win more friends, there is the setting out, the meeting of new acquaintances, the doing of specific acts, and the getting of desired responses. Here the picture has, of necessity, to move, so must be run over and over like a short piece of film. It falls under our heading of "meditation" rather than concentration, but can be reduced and condensed in time and covered with a single suggestion command, such as "Make friends." (We will come back to this shortening process a little later.)

Tests by the Associates also brought out sharply the fact that mental images of the visual type may be difficult for some to construct, while impressions based on some of the other senses are comparatively easy. Some found it easier and better to imagine auditory or tactile impressions and concentrate upon them. Taste and smell, or a combination of sensory impressions, helped on the making of a mental image which was not of the visual type.

The intensity of sensation with which mental impressions can be reproduced varies greatly. Some can actually cause in themselves the sensation of seeing a color, or of hearing a sound. Usually there are certain better loved colors or sounds which the low self will recall and reproduce better than others.

What was learned, by and large, was that we all have our strong and weak points when it comes to making the idea structures to be used in self-suggestion. The beginner needs to run through some tests to determine which are his strong points and which his weak ones.

If one tries concentrating on one color after another, it will soon be apparent whether one color comes clearer than the others, or whether the low self is able to hand up only memories of different colors rather than the sensation of actually seeing them. If one finds a face is grey instead of in color when recalled and held as something to concentrate upon for practice, that shows a certain lack of visual ability. It may indicate that some of the other senses should be tried in making experimental images. The touch of the fingers on the cheek may be recalled and may bring back a vivid imaging, or the picturing of a flower may be made suddenly easy if its perfume and the feel of its petals are remembered, along with its color.

The low self, of course, is right with us every step of the way in making the images, and its cooperation is something to be courted, and, when obtained, acknowledged with praise. Things which are hated or disliked are poor to use as images, although old hurts and fears are easier to hold longer in concentration. They may upset the low self badly and make it shy away from the whole matter of self-suggestion. Happy and loved and pleasant memories are best for practice, and by using them, the low self will soon come to enjoy the work and help with valuable enthusiasm. If it learns to expect happy and pleasant results, and if pleasant things, which do not run counter to habits, such, for example, as smoking, are worked on in the mood field for a time, the low self will learn to help make mental images with pleasure and confidence.

Learning to concentrate and meditate, as we use these terms, is hardest for those who need most to get the low self in hand. With some the low self is headstrong like a willful child, which cannot be made to pay attention for more than a moment before it scampers away to indulge in its own play devices. If the concentration time is less than twenty seconds, when using the pulsation-of-image method, one needs to take time for daily practice. The time of holding an image can be gradually lengthened and the low self brought under control. The average time of from one to two minutes for such concentration is good enough for self-suggestion purposes of a very effective kind.

The meditation form of moving image should be something that can be held for at least three minutes, but the low self may tire and run off with the show. It may present pictures of its own which have not been dictated by the middle self in its endeavor to make a set of general images covering larger actions and situations, such as the one of making friends.

To strengthen the idea structure of a thing concentrated or meditated upon, is very simple. Patanjali wrote wisely that meditation is based on the meditations which have gone before. In other words, one recalls from the memory store, with the aid of the low self, the idea structures already worked upon, then works them over still more. In this way, as in learning to memorize a poem, the structures become familiar and strong and take on more and more vital force and "will" charge. After a little practice the ideas can be recalled instantly and one can go over them without half trying because the low self is beginning to do part of the work. But to let the low self do all the work will be to stop laying the heavy and all-important charge of "will" force on the structures, and that is to be avoided by carefully attending to the work of going over and over the ideas.

It has been the experience of a number of experimenters that very often, if the middle self is firmly determined to follow through and get the low self to help while making a drive to bring about certain better conditions, the low self will begin to react to the charged ideas even before the time comes to relax it consciously and give it the suggestion.

Things like the yawn, or sleep, or awakening at a certain time in the morning, are tasks which the low self already has been accustomed to care for. In these it is often necessary only to make a single strong idea and dwell on it as a picturing of what is desired, in order to have the low self react without the formality of giving the suggestion. All it may need is to hear the middle self say, "Tonight we will sleep deeply and soundly. We will have a really profound and enjoyable and refreshing sleep, with pleasant dreams. In the morning we will awaken exactly at six o'clock and we will be feeling ever so refreshed and ready to begin the day." Next to the yawn, this suggestion of better sleep is the easiest thing for the beginner to demonstrate.

With practice one can begin to construct a trigger or release word, which when spoken or thought, will recall the entire idea structure and hand it over to the low self with its charges, causing reactions to begin at once. The entire picture of a fine and restful night of sleep can be shortened gradually in the recall-and-strengthen process by using fewer words in describing the good sleep. It can be reduced to something like, "Sound sleep, and awakening at six". If several meanings are assigned to a single word, that word can be used as a trigger word, but usually there is no need for such great brevity unless one may frequently be thrown into positions where the low self has to be reminded by a single word what it must do or refrain from doing. The old idea of counting to ten before letting the temper show, might serve as an example. If this were used as a suggestion and the formula reduced to a single word, "Count", it might start the desired reaction in the low self on the instant under emergency conditions.

The relationship of the middle and low selves is a very close one, and, normally it is a happy one. But if a "house is divided against itself", the pulling and hauling is very destructive. The low self is to be loved and cherished, brought along patiently and carefully. It is not to be hammered over the head with suggestion, but is to be told what glowing things you are undertaking and how fine it will be for the low self to do everything possible in its department of life to help bring about the new and happier state of things. If the middle self can work up real enthusiasm over the change which is to be made, and can match this enthusiasm with determination - which is the exercising of the "will" - the work will be half accomplished before it is begun. It will remain only for the middle self to get the low self to relax once a day and then to turn over to it the heavily charged ideas in the form of a suggestion. With the giving of the suggestion day after day, the trigger words can be decided upon, and the results will grow more and more apparent.

One thing which must not be forgotten is that when a suggestion is given to the low self, one must not be an Indian giver and demand the idea back at once so that it can be mulled over and worried as a dog worries a bone. The idea is to be given bodily to the low self, and then the middle self is to stop thinking about it - take its hands off and keep them off - until the next period of suggestion. Let the low self have its head and work out a way to begin to make the appropriate reactions. One does not plant a seed, then dig it up daily to see if it is growing. The low self is the moist soil, and the seed will have been planted in it after making the soil as receptive as is humanly possible. After the planting there must be faith that the soil will do its part and that the seed will do its. If the middle self has full confidence and faith in the outcome, the low self will also have faith and will do wonders to make the seed grow. But if there is doubt on the part of the middle self, that doubt will be shared by the low self and it will lose heart and not try to grow the seed. Self-suggestion calls for team work. It calls for a happily carried out and united effort - for integration of purposes, desires and determinations.

If integration and full, smoothly working cooperation between the low and middle selves is brought about, little difficulty will be experienced in including the High Self in the team and so completing the the normal state of integration which, in all ages, has been the goal of Huna and of closely related systems such as Christianity, Gnosticism and early Yoga. One day it will become the goal of philosophy. Then we shall have perfected a philosophical system which will match what we cannot help but observe all about us - not the preconceived notions which the philosophers may have borrowed or evolved in hit-and-miss fashion.

Chapter 6

Once one has come to understand the theory behind concentration and meditation (as we are using
the two terms) and has experimented to see how best
to create mental thought form images to be used as
suggestions, the theory behind the charging of the
idea structures with vital force and "will" power
needs to be taken up in more detail.

The history of Mesmer's "animal magnetism" is
one that has run anything but smoothly. Because it
was not "electricity", as this force was coming to be
known, and because Braid had taught that tiring the
eyes brought on a receptive state much like normal
sleep, in which suggestions were accepted by the
subject, there was a general discarding of mesmerism and of all tentative belief that vital force might
be involved in hypnosis. However, one school of
thought was developing in which it was taught that the
hypnotist must "dominate" his subject with his "will".

The "domination" theory rapidly came into favor
even though no one could say what "will" might be. It
seemed to the onlooker that the hypnotist was impos-
ing his "will" on his subject in order to make him do
the outlandish things which amused audiences in the
theaters. A cult grew up quite aside from the field
of Braidian suggestion, and the new leaders wrote
books and sold courses telling of the wonders of the
human "will" and how to use it.

The "will" was not spoken of as vital force or power because even weak invalids had been seen to be able to exert a "will" power sufficient to lay all relatives and doctors by the heels. The flavor of the legendary "evil eye", or the fire-flashing eye of the born commander of men permeated the writings. To use the "will" power was to pull oneself up by the boot straps in some magical fashion which could not be explained, but which was proclaimed possible. One could do it if one just would, but "do or die" was the motto for a surprisingly long time after those testing the validity of the system found it lacking.

In a book written in 1894, titled "The Will Power", its author, J. Milner Fothergill, M.D., wrote on his opening page, "What the will is, is a matter upon which metaphysicians have not yet been able to make up their minds, after all the attention bestowed on the subject; and when they have come to some conclusion, either of agreement or fixity of disagreement, the results will have no practical value..... Will is one of the 'little men who stand behind us', mind, soul, spirit, will, intangible something, revealed to us, - how?..... Yet we never hesitate to use these words, nor is there any difficulty about their being comprehended by others..... a man may have moderate abilities, and yet attain great success because he possesses a firm will..... It is the will which enables a man to carry out what the intellect devises."

Dr. Fothergill filled many pages with accounts of men, good and bad, famous and infamous, who had made their places in history through the use of will power. He concluded his book with a summing up, "The will may not endow a man with talents or capacities: but it does one very important thing, it enables him to make the best, the very most of his powers........If this little book enables one single reader to plant his feet firmer in the ground in fighting the battle of life, it will not have been written in vain."

Even without the knowledge of what composes the will power of which he wrote, Dr. Fothergill hit one nail squarely on the head when he disclosed the dismal truth that most people refuse to act even after having the wonderful benefits of the use of the will power explained to them. He was very right. It is not enough to show that something is good. One has to make people want it badly enough to rouse themselves and start going after it. The desire must be equally strong in the low self, and this is where self-suggestion comes in, as we shall eventually see.

Psychologists have long argued as to the nature of desire and of the inner drive which causes the individual to strive to get the thing desired. One may desire something greatly, but make no effort to get it.

The dictionaries define "will" as wish or desire, but stumble over the difference and say that an "act of consciousness" is added in some way to the wish or desire to make it become a "will" to fulfill the wish.

In the year 2,000 A. D. we may possibly read this definition: "Will: to want something and then to go after it."

In his very excellent, "New Dictionary of Psychology", the learned Philip Lawrence Harriman exposes the lack of real information in the careful definition, "Will: a controversial term of ambiguous connotation. In rational psychology, will is a central concept; in radical behaviorism, it is a label for the triumph of the strongest stimulus; in philosophical psychology, it is a mental faculty. Many contemporary psychologists consider the matter to lie outside the province of psychology, though there is a strong implication of determinism in modern psychology."

"Determinism" is the Freudian theory that physical or mental conditions force us to do things and that we have no freedom of choice - so, no "will". In their "Freud, Dictionary of Psychoanalysis", edited by Dr. Nandor Fodor and Frank Gaynor, one may search in vain for any definition of "will" or mention of the theory of "determinism".

In their "Hypnotism Handbook", Cooke and Van Vogt come near to the Huna idea of the vital force charge laid on a suggestion thought form. They say that each word spoken by the hypnotist in the administration of suggestion has "energy" and that upon this "energy" and upon the correct understanding of the meaning of the word hinges the getting or not getting of results. That states the principle, even if no reason is given as to why there is energy in the words, or how it gets there.

Searching through Powis Hoult's "A Dictionary of Some Theosophical Terms," one finds no definition of "will", but is helpfully referred to the material under the heading of "Yoga". Under that heading the several main schools of Yoga are listed, but the only word which might be used to indicate the "will" is the Sanskrit, "yama", which is given the meaning of a "restraining" action. This is typical of the very brief and indirect meanings of the words used in early Yoga writings. One must see that all acts of "will" which restrain the low self from doing the

66

wrong things (which is the basic or beginning step in Yoga), must be balanced by compensating acts to cause the low self to begin doing the right things. There are always two sides to every question, and there are usually two balanced meanings, or positive and negative meanings behind most simple statements of Yoga principles.

Owing to the lack of a suitable understanding of the nature of the "will" in psychological circles, we are forced to turn back to the system of psychology discovered centuries ago by the ancestors of the people we now know as the Polynesians. Only in their Huna lore can one find the understanding that is needed to throw light on the problem.

The kahunas, or native priests of pre-Polynesian times, very evidently invented a special vocabulary to use to describe the elements which they found to make up a man. There were, in the ten elements which they recognized and named, three which were part of the life force or "will" - the three "manas".

The reason there were three words used, was that man is composed of three selves, and that each self has a "will" of its very own, just as each has its own form of thinking ability, and its own type of shadowy body.

If we accept the Huna discovery as correct, we can then go on to ask how the three "wills" of the three selves differ, how they may be made to give a single drive in one selected direction, and how "will" and desire differ.

Let us first consider the "will" of the low self. This self is an animal self living in an animal body. It may desire something but make no effort to get it. Or it may decide to do or not to do something, appar-

67

ently without the emotion of desire being aroused, and make a great effort to have its own way. A balky mule is the prize example of the "will" of an animal at work. The mule decides not to move. No desire for food can coax it forward. Beating cannot move it. To all intents and purposes it wants nothing, unless we might say that it wants to refuse to move. Its stubborn resistance is vast and amazing. On the other hand, a mule may wish to get into a green field, and may go to surprising lengths to break through a fence and accomplish its purpose.

The low or animal self has the lesser or deductive power of reason. It reasons from what it remembers, then arrives at a conclusion, and from this its desire and "will" are stirred into action. Everything depends on the memories of former experiences. These are thought form ideas and the reaction to them depends on how heavily charged they were with vital force when the original events took place that gave rise to the memories used in later reasoning. To this must be added the instinctive needs which cause desires and "will" drives to satisfy them.

The strength of a desire or of a "will" drive depends upon the degree to which an original event or experience has left its imprint. Great emotions cause strong and "will" filled memories. These, when recalled, will cause the same emotions and drives to awaken, even if not quite as strong as in the original experience. That is the key to everything in suggestion - the more a set of ideas is charged with vital force as it is formed, the more of a reaction it will cause when recalled as a memory.

Next consider the Huna information about the

middle self and its "will". This self, as has been said, lives as a guest in the physical body which is owned and controlled by the low self. It has no power to remember and must depend on the low self to care for all memories and give them back when wanted. It can produce no emotions for itself. Its two talents are, first, that of using the superior or inductive form of reason, and, secondly, it can take the vital force from the body (where it is manufactured by the low self) and use it to make its own grade of "will" force.

The "will" force of the middle self has what might be likened to a higher potential, in speaking of electricity. Because of this, it can overcome any lower potential of the "will" such as that of the low self.

On the other hand, the low self has the ability to avoid control by the more potent "will" of the middle self. This is largely because the middle self must charge ideas with its powerful "will" force and try to get the low self to take them as something to be put into the memory storage, and also spur it to react to them on contact by the shock of the heavy charge. The low self may be said to balk and refuse to react to highly charged ideas if they cover something which it fears or disagrees with - something which runs counter to its own preferred sets of similar ideas.

The two selves, living in the same body and being so closely interdependent for mutual assistance, share the same emotions as well as memories, and the middle self is often swept away by the strength of the emotions of fear or anger or love generated by the low self. It is, therefore, much easier and better for the two selves to work in harmony, and as the middle self is more evolved and more intelligent, it must take the lead in harmonizing the relationship. It must be the wise and kindly guide. It is the older brother who is, or should be, its "brother's keeper".

The High Self, who also draws on the low for its supply of life or vital force, has also its own superior way of thinking as well as its own desires and potential of "will". The "will" of the low self is mesmeric and may be thought of as a great club. That of the middle self may be likened to the bullet shot from a gun, and that of the High Self to a lightning bolt.

The language used by the discoverers of Huna is the only one known today which contains words to name all the different elements in the system. The language, quite evidently, was constructed for the purpose of containing these words and hiding their true meanings under an overload of one or more common meanings. Some complicated Huna ideas were hidden by symbol words. For instance, the word "water" was the symbol for the vital force and for its use in any potential of strength as the "will" by the three individual selves.

To understand what the kahunas discovered concerning the several elements used in mesmeric suggestion or self-suggestion, is not difficult. One has but to consult the secondary and symbolic meanings in the words they used. (The Hawaiian dialect of the Polynesian tongue is replete with such meanings.)

We may see how the kahunas looked upon suggestion by observing the fact that their main words for it are "kumu manao", meaning "exchange thoughts", and showing that there was the belief that the operator caused the low self of the subject to accept a suggested idea to replace one which was to be taken in trade or removed. In self-suggestion the trade is between the low and middle selves, and the low self must be made to desire what is offered before it will be willing to give up what it has already in exchange.

They called the things exchanged, "seeds", and these stood for the highly vitalized sets of ideas used to be implanted by the middle self into the low self as suggestions. The "seed" was also "the likeness of a thing", or, in other words, a mold or shadowy body duplication of some original thing. It was not, for example, the actual condition in which more friends were being made, but it was a wonderful little picture of the condition, and, as such, it commanded and also guided the low self when used as a suggestion. It helped create the condition of which it is the tiny, invisible likeness.

The relaxation needed to quiet the body and mind of the low self so that it will accept suggestion "likenesses", was also given a name. It was the same word used for seed, "ano", but a different one of its several alternate meanings was employed. This is the meaning of "a sacred place of stillness". This is again a symbol. It symbolizes the relaxed and quiet condition in which the low self is made receptive. It is the receptiveness of one kneeling expectantly before a shrine, waiting confidently for a requested blessing to be bestowed. No more beautiful and significant symbol than this could have been selected to describe the ideal state into which the low self must be induced to fall. It is a state of trust and faith as well as of expectancy. It is a quiet emotional state of great value when suggestion is to be given.

To make a set of ideas, charge it with the "will" force of the middle self, and then cause the low self

71

to accept it as a suggestion, was a three-part act which was called "manao" or "nanao". The common meanings of these words, together with their secondary meanings and symbol values, tell us what the kahunas considered necessary when giving suggestion. The words also provide some sidelight information on the nature of the low self.

To make a rather mixed set of meanings more easily grasped, the process can be given in stages. First, one must be able to hold the low self, and it is described in this pair of words and their root meanings as "slippery" and hard to find or to hold, once found. It is a self which may easily lead one astray or cause one to turn aside instead of driving straight ahead to grip and control it with suggestion. It is described as a self living in a dark hole where it cannot be seen and where the hand is thrust in to try to find it. Once found, the suggestion must be forced upon it, as food is forced on one refusing to eat.

Secondly, the words indicate that one MUST THINK HARD, which symbolizes the intense concentration on the ideas while they are being charged with the "will" force and made ready for use as suggestions. The root of the word (mana) names the basic vital force so necessary to the making of thought structures and "will" charges.

The ancient kahunas usually invented two or three words with the same general sets of meanings lest one might get lost or its meanings changed with the passage of time. In keeping with this precautionary custom, they invented a second word, "hahao", for suggestion. Its meaning, as given in the dictionaries, is literal and direct. It means, "to suggest

72

something to the mind of another". But in the roots
of the word the kahunas took care to tell how such
suggesting was to be done. The roots give the meaning of "to breathe hard", which is the symbol of accumulating extra vital force to use in making the suggestion ideas and charging them. This is a companion activity to go with the "hard thinking".

The root "hao" means "to place a little thing into
a larger thing", and this tells us that the tiny thought
structures of the suggestion, once made ready, are
to be given to the low self to place with its other remembered ideas in the large place where all memories are stored.

The word for "faith" or "to believe" is very important in any discussion of suggestion, and for this
meaning we must go back again to the word "manao".
Not only does it mean "to think", but it means "to
believe."

To sum up, the kahunas instructed those wishing
to use suggestion:

TO THINK HARD

TO BREATHE HARD, and

TO BELIEVE COMPLETELY.

Mention has been made of the accumulation of
extra vital force by hard breathing. This needs a
fuller explanation.

For our purposes we may simply say that to accumulate extra vital force to pour into the suggestion
idea structure and to use to make the force of "will"
to add also, we need to:

(1) Take over the breathing job from the low self
and begin breathing more heavily. This will hold the
attention of the low self and, if we expect the vital
force to be built up rapidly above the normal supply,

the low self will use up a little more of the food elements in the body and give us the extra charge. All extra vital force is stored in the shadowy body of the low self and is right at hand as we think and create mental images and charge them heavily.

(2) Keep on breathing more deeply and controlling the breath as the middle self. There are several reasons why this impresses and holds the attention of the low self, but we need not go into them here. While performing this part of the work - the breathing, or "ha", one also begins to "think hard". To think hard is to exert the "will" of the middle self to make the low self stand by attentively and allow us to concentrate the whole attention on the task of making the mental images, or, if they were made in earlier sittings, to recall and review them carefully, attentively and strongly in every detail, trying to charge them while so doing. The "hard thinking" or concentration needs to be "pulsed", that is, let the idea go for an instant, then take it up again. It is a process similar to winking the eyes when gazing with fixed attention at some interesting object or spectacle. The momentary wink allows the needed pause to restore the mana or force used up in the gazing. The concentration on the suggestion ideas will build the vital force into them and make the charge larger and stronger. The force of the "will" is added at the same time by holding and reaffirming the determination that the idea embodied in the suggestion shall become a fact in living - an actual and lasting condition, this being greatly desired and the determination to bring it about unwaveringly backed by faith, and with no slightest doubt of the outcome. Such an idea, charged and held with the desire for it built to a high

74

point, then overlaid with the fullest determination to bring it to realization, has in it the ingredient of the middle self "will". This ingredient will remain in and with the suggestion as long as the middle self keeps the desire and determination running strong. The low self will be moved to do what it alone can do to help along with the plan, and in many things it will do almost all of the actual work, once it is given suggestion in this way often enough to keep the charge replenished and gradually increased from day to day.

These things are very simple, but because they are very new to most of us when we first become acquainted with them, they may appear very complicated and even difficult. This newness passes after a few readings of explanations and after testing out a few of the steps, then trying in a small way on something which is rather easy to put through, such as changing the attitude toward others so that more and more friends will be made, or brightening up or raising the average mood level.

To make a beginning, the use of the self-suggestion method starts with the middle self, which is you, and with the exertion of a little of your "will". You will have to find some way to make yourself desire to have the benefit of the method which is being laid before you. If you can find just a little desire, this can be changed to a little "will", and that will be a decision to give it a try. Once you have passed that first hurdle, the going becomes easier and enthusiasm builds. Soon you will be involved in the most delightful and rewarding part of the process, the part in which you will have the fascinating and wonderful experience of being able to contact your own High Self and invite it to aid and direct you in all things.

Chapter 7

After you have learned the knack of concentration and that of charging the ideas to be used for suggestion purposes, you will be ready to take up the
matter of teaching the low self to relax.

The Huna theories offer a much needed explanation to tell us why the low self accepts suggestion
more readily when we are physically relaxed and
when the mental activities of the low self have been
slowed down, even if not completely stopped.

It is the matter of the charge of vital force again.
If the low self and its body are both normally active,
there is a heavy charge of vital force in its shadowy
body. This force is not of the same grade as that used by the middle self, but we can picture two heavily charged batteries set together and their terminals
connected with the idea that the battery with the
stronger charge will release some of its electricity
to fill the other. If both batteries are at the same
level of charge, there will be no interchange.

Huna tells us that administering suggestion is a
process of planting a powerfully charged thought form
idea in the mind of the low self, the middle self doing
the planting.

If the low self is as heavily charged as the middle self, it tends to reject the offered thought form
ideas. But if it is relaxed in body and mind it be-

76

comes negative. If the middle self and the suggestion structure remain positive, the low self seems even to attract the suggestion to itself and to begin at once to react to it.

When the low self is relaxed, it ceases to need more than a minimum charge, and because of this, the middle self can draw much of the vital force to its center of consciousness to help it to "think hard" and pour a charge of added "will" force into the suggestion structure.

The original kahunas must have thought that anyone would know how to relax, for the word they used for "to relax" was "hoolulu" which also means "to sow or plant seeds" - the symbol of planting the tiny forms of the suggestion idea in the low self. However, the kahunas, by this combining of meanings left no doubt that the low self was to be relaxed and that something must be planted.

The first step in bringing about low self relaxation of body and mind must be taken by the middle self. Once more it takes over the handling of the voluntary muscles, just as in taking over the breathing action. The low self in the body is commanded by the use of the "will" to obey, or conform, to the middle self's mental picture of going to a comfortable chair or couch and making the body comfortable. That done, the mental picture is held over the low self as a command to cause it to stop thinking, or at least to slow down its rate of thinking. The kahunas had a phrase meaning "relax the mind", which translates, "relax the intestines", in which the intestines symbolize, as always, the low self, so we know that it is not the middle self which is to be relaxed. It is to increase its activities even as it uses the "will" to

77

make the low self ease up on its activities. The use of the "will" to command the low self always has a little of the element of suggestion in it whether we realize it or not. We command the body to act, and we take over the voluntary muscles and start the action, usually starting or triggering a habit of previously learned chain type reaction. For example, the low self, once started, will turn the eyes to see where there is a comfortable chair, move the body to it and cause it to sit down, lean back, and find a comfortable position.

When we wish to relax the body for a purpose other than that of rest or sleep, we are apt to run head-on into the habit reactions of the low self which get triggered off as we give it the idea of relaxing. It cannot use inductive reason, so is easily confused when it does not know exactly what is wanted or why it is wanted. Also, it may have ideas of its own, as, in this instance, that it does not need rest or sleep at this time. If the middle self insists, the low self will usually try to oblige, after some objection. It will rest obediently, but is apt to fidget and to let its thoughts go wandering off. If the idea of relaxation is associated with that of sleep, it may obediently put one to sleep, and that upsets all the plans, for sleep uncouples the two selves and cuts off the supply of vital force from the middle self so that it ceases to function almost entirely.

The hypnotists, under Dr. Braid's leadership, learned that the needed relaxation could be obtained by tiring the eyes so much that the low self would rest of its own accord, and in resting, would fall into the relaxed state in which suggestion is most readily accepted. The eyes use up most of the vital force when they are put under a muscular strain, and when they tire and close, the type of relaxation that goes ahead of natural sleep cames easily. Looking with the eyes strained upward at a bright point of light or at a whirling disk on which has been painted a spiral line, tires the eyes quickly and tends to cause relaxation in modern hypnotic practice.

But the eyes are only a part of the body. In addition to tiring them by trying for a few moments to stare up at a point between the eyebrows, which is an experiment one can try, there are other ways to be employed to tire and relax the whole body.

The "Decubitus" method of relaxation worked out by Dr. Frederick Pierce can be used. This method should be used following or before or as a part of the eye tiring exercise. It consists of tiring the main muscles of the body, then relaxing them by letting go. A tired muscle will relax far more completely and far sooner than one not first made to use up its supply of vital force by working under some strain.

Dr. Pierce advised taking the legs, one at a time, then the arms, then the body and neck. Each was to be lifted, or the muscles tightened and held as in lifting until they tired slightly, after which the limb or other part was relaxed, pressed against the chair or couch for a moment and then let go entirely while the mental command was given to relax completely.

A "one shot" method is to tense all the muscles throughout the body or to stretch and yawn vastly and hold the stretch until slightly tired, then let go all over and command the low self to relax.

When testing out these methods, it has been found good to examine different parts of the body to see whether there is any remaining muscular tense-

79

ness. The hands, face and chest muscles are often-est found still a little tense and in need of conscious effort to make them let go completely. Or, the eyes may have opened wide, after having been first re-laxed, in which case they are to be partly drooped or closed, not fully closed, however, as that would invite the low self to put one to sleep and so upset the apple cart filled with waiting suggestion-ideas.

After the relaxation, the body is allowed to sit or recline inert and the low self is watched and made to stop churning up thoughts - often thought trains connected with the activities of the day. These trains can be stopped or slowed down and they will usually vanish as soon as one begins slowly to increase the breathing rate and to hold the mental picture of draw-ing all the vital force into the middle self center of consciousness and adding to it while one recalls the ideas one had been working to perfect, thinking them over backward and forward - "thinking hard" about them. This will be concentration and will automati-cally add the "will" charge and command to the struc-tures. In a matter of from ten seconds for the ex-perienced person, or a minute or so for the beginner, the suggestion thought form cluster and its charge of "will" force will be ready for planting.

The planting is done by telling the low self si-lently, in a whisper, or, if no one is near to hear, in a normal voice, to take the mental image on which you have been working and care for it carefully be-cause all the things in it are going to be very helpful, very delightful, very useful, very important and very necessary to bring about. Command it quietly to be-gin to do all it can to bring about the desired condi-tion, and promise that you will do all you can. Be

80

sure you mean it and that you keep your promise. If you leave it all to the low self and begin to do things contrary to what you plan, the low self will fall back quickly into its old and habitual way of doing things, and the suggestion with its charge of force will probably be disposed of by hitching it to some other set of remembered ideas and muddling them both.

These muddled suggestions, when strong, may cause the low self to react in strange and irrational ways in unexpected fields if not kept under attentive watch by the middle self. In case you, the middle self, decide to change or cancel a suggestion and give up trying to bring about the better mood or whatever it may be that you have started to try to get, do not leave the suggestion lying around in the memory store room like a time bomb whose firing pin may be pulled inadvertently by the low self in trying to dispose of it.

Take up the idea to be cancelled and think hard and long to picture it as cancelled. See it as something no longer wanted. Tell the low self in a regular relaxation-suggestion session that the other suggestion is being changed back to a simple memory of something once desired, but no longer wanted. It is now only a simple memory to be stored in the usual way. Make a mental effort to draw the forces from the ideas and to picture them as cancelled.

If a suggestion covers something which the low self can do or bring about all by itself, and you cannot help, do not let go your hold entirely when you give the suggestion daily to the low self. Tie a thread of shadowy body substance to it by holding the attitude of quiet expectancy whenever the matter embodied in the suggestion is recalled. Also, as the suggestion comes to mind, say to the low self, "That's right. Keep working on it to bring it about. Good!" A little praise is a great help, and confident expectation is a steadying and guiding influence.

After a period of relaxation it is well to tell the low self that the very pleasing and valuable little session is over and to command it to get back to the work of the day, full of energy and ready to undertake anything with enthusiasm. This is a valuable step to take because the place where suggestion begins to work and where it leaves off is hard to determine. Also, it varies with the individual. Some of us are very suggestible and some not. It is always safe to put in what the Scientologists call "the cancellor".

The hypnotist is always careful to suggest a full recovery from the receptive condition at a definite time, even if a posthypnotic suggestion is left in the low self of the subject to be reacted to later. Usually the command runs something like this, "When I count back from five to zero you will be wide awake and will feel fine." The reverse count is made and the subject comes out of the trance, be it slight or deep.

In mesmerism, if no suggestion is given, the subject comes back to normal as soon as the stunning charge of vital force has been absorbed and distributed through the shadowy body of the subject. There is, in such a case, no need for cancelling because no suggestion has been given. Ordinarily, it has been found by hypnotists, suggestions begin to lose their power in a week or ten days. Patients under treatment to prevent attacks in epilepsy, or to prevent suffering from the pains of chronic illness, must have suggestions renewed periodically.

The difference between suggestion administered

by a hypnotist and by oneself in self-suggestion, is mainly a matter of whether the operator's middle self or one's own makes the charged set of ideas and plants them in the relaxed and receptive low self. In the case of the hypnotist, he has to use either telepathy or words to implant a suggestion. While rapport is sometimes continued telepathically after a session, when the operator wishes it to continue, the work is largely done by the low self as it reacts steadily to the suggestion structures which it has accepted. As a rule, there is no more use of telepathy after an "aka" or shadowy thread of connection has been established by first contact between operator and subject than there is between two strangers who chance to meet, shake hands, and go their separate ways.

In discussing the details of mesmerism and self-suggestion, it comes to appear to be a complicated and difficult mechanism, but it is really very simple. Let us review the few and easy steps which need to be taken in using self-suggestion.

1. Decide what you are going to suggest.
2. Think hard about it to make strong ideas.
3. Breathe hard and accumulate extra vital force while thinking hard about the suggestion ideas to charge them with force.
4. Relax the low self in mind and body.
5. Speak the suggestion silently or aloud to it.
6. Finish by telling the low self that the session is over and for it to stop relaxing and take up the work of the day alertly.
7. Expect the low self to react. When you recall the suggestion, do it placidly until the next session, when you will again become

very positive in repeating the suggestion.

8. In case it becomes necessary or good to delay or even give up a planned effort to accomplish some aim, explain the reasons to the low self, then make the mental picture of the project being delayed or even given up completely. Charge the idea and administer it in self-suggestion in the regular way. Do not let the effort go by default lest the old suggestion structures worry the low self and cause a mental clutter. A mental house needs to be kept neat and clean and well ordered at all times.

Chapter 8

We come now to the place toward which we have been working by learning the theory and practice of self-suggestion. Here we crown the achievements, and pass from the great earthly benefits which self-suggestion can give into the world of pure magic and the miraculous - into the world of "PRAYER".

But PRAYER, within the meaning of Huna, is a very different thing from prayer with the meaning given it today in the churches. In Huna we have a knowledge of the three selves making up the man. In Huna-type prayer we find all three selves have a part in the prayer, and that each has special things to do which cannot be done by the others. If each does its part and uses its unique natural ability expertly, a miracle is possible. If only one self tries to pray, nothing happens.

Self-suggestion is the way by which we can cause all three of the selves of the triune man to work as a balanced and perfect team toward a single accomplishment.

The experimenters who are leading in the field of autoconditioning and autosuggestion are becoming vaguely aware that there should be this crowning step in the art of using suggestion to bring the low self into full agreement and cooperation (integration) with the middle self, then with something still higher.

Dr. Hornell Hart, in his lectures on the subject as well as in his writings, strongly urges that the religious aspect of the process be stressed. He describes the aim as, ... "to live joyously and to create the kind of personality capable of profound service to our fellow men, to transcend the life we now live, reach out into the spiritual potentialities of life with courage and creative faith." This is a splendid aim and goal, but the student must turn to Huna to find the step-by-step directions needed to accomplish the work of putting the "potentialities" to practical use.

Dr. Rolf Alexander, who clings to the Freudian "id, ego and superego" in contrast to the ancient Polynesian low self, middle self and High Self, offers a method by which one learns to work with the superego. This is the method he has named "self realization". It resembles in flavor the Zen system of attaining "enlightenment" or "realization", but retains the vagueness of the original superego concept even while enlarging it.

Dr. Alexander falls back on the idea that we are all living in a continuous state of hypnotization in which the events of our lives and our surroundings act as hypnotic suggestions to bind and shape the ego, preventing it from realizing the world of reality which surrounds us. The recommended remedy is the breaking free from the hypnotized state and the emergence into the normal state in which the "true" and "real" are sensed and the superego begins to guide one's life. This condition is described as "salvation", as "liberation", and as the complete integration of the three parts of the Freudian self. It goes considerably farther toward metaphysics than the accepted system of Freud permits, but still falls far short of recognizing the High Self as the end and aim of the autohypnotic efforts.

Some years ago in New England, a mesmerist traveled about and demonstrated Mesmer's healing methods. A man named Quimby became interested, learned to use mesmerism, and set himself up as a healer, evolving in the process a set of theories to explain what happens in the process of such healing. From his theories, which touched a little on religion and metaphysics, there evolved New Thought and Christian Science.

In New Thought circles one of the leaders was Judge Troward. He had served in India and had absorbed some of the concepts of Yoga and Vedanta. Hypnotism had come to the fore by the time he began to write, and he delightedly fastened upon the strange new theory of "suggestion" in building for himself a new set of explanations to cover that step which is to be taken as we move from the physical to the super-physical - from the low and middle self realm to in-include that of the High Self.

Oddly enough, Judge Troward failed to see in the miraculous answers obtained through prayers the evidence of a Higher Power. He carefully avoided the older concept of a close and personal God made in man's image, and, avoiding the Superconscious entirely, proposed a "UNIVERSAL SUBCONSCIOUS". This was, perhaps, less surprising than it would look on the surface. What had impressed him most was the apparently verified fact that when one "held the thought" long and well, after the budding New Thought method, one built up a mysterious compulsive force which in some way influenced something more powerful than man, causing it to bring into reality the thing so pictured and demanded. The Yoga tradition was that the miraculous could be brought about by concentration, but in this there was little to offer scientific backing. On the other hand, hypnosis and suggestion were being generally accepted.

His postulated "Universal Subconscious" was a natural deduction for one following through from mesmerism to suggestion and reaching out toward the miraculous in the field of answered prayer. He had reasoned that a Superconscious of universal size and creative power must be too high to be controlled by the thoughts of men, so the thing that certainly was seen to accept control, must be similar to the subconscious of man. Ergo! A Universal Subconscious must be the answer And it must also have miraculous power, being part of the Superconscious. The only flaw which developed in this theory which was widely hailed and accepted in New Thought, was that the Universal Subconscious so often refused to obey "thought-held" suggestion.

This revolt against the older religious concept of prayer has been going on for some time, largely because of the failure to get results by orthodox prayer methods. Something "scientific" was demanded which could be used to get unfailing results. And, it should not be necessary for one to be kind, generous or good, as in orthodox circles, to be able to tip up the Horn of Plenty by some "action of mind", so that blessings could rain down. Many felt that God should stop playing favorites and answering the prayers of some while ignoring the prayers of others.

As the new religions springing from this revolt were partly founded on the old Quimby healing demonstrations, healing remained one of the things most desired and expected. However, it was always very discouraging to a "practitioner" to have a client fail to become well, then go to a "natural healer" who might get excellent results from simple orthodox prayer.

But all is not easy to explain in orthodox circles. Some become famed for their "power in prayer", and others, often living seemingly far more worthy and devoted lives, suffer tragedies which prayer seldom alleviates.

Obviously, our knowledge of prayer is badly in need of overhauling.

A few famous psychologists have viewed this sad contradiction of current religious speculations, and have written learnedly about it. William James, in his book, "Varieties of Religious Experiences", made a classical contribution to the subject. In later years in his book, "Man the Unknown", Dr. Alexis Carrel gave the world a study of the miraculous answers to prayer occurring down the years at the shrine at Lourdes, in France, where those who came to pray for others were oftenest healed themselves - an odd state of affairs which contradicts all current beliefs and speculations.

Two features of effective prayer may be seen to be outstanding. (1) There must be a strong emotion of desire aroused in making a prayer, and (2) there must be confident expectation or faith that the prayer will be answered.

It makes little difference to whom the prayers are addressed so long as it is some Higher Being. This may be God, as named in any language or conceived in any religion. It can be prayer to any Savior in any religion, such as Jesus or Buddha. It can be prayer addressed to saints or ancestors.

An additional discovery has been made, but its recognition has been so slow that today it is almost completely overlooked. This is the discovery that mesmerism, coupled with prayer, could and did bring about healings verging on the miraculous. We have already seen that Col. Henry S. Olcott, active in the early years of the Theosophical Society, had explored this angle. In his writings he described his experience in healing over fifty paralytics in Ceylon, saying that he had made use of the faith of the patients in Buddha. He encouraged them to believe that when they asked it, the Buddha would heal them. This brought in a strong element of prayer to add some ingredient (not discussed or defined) to the mesmeric force exerted by Col. Olcott. As there was the intention to heal mingled with the expectation of being healed, the element of suggestion was very strong, even if not recognized as part of the process. The combination of ingredients worked wonders - wonders which still puzzle the modern hypnotists who cannot understand how mesmerism can bring about healing results which they cannot begin to duplicate.

For the moment let us leave the line of thought which we have been following to consider a form of healing which is too important to be overlooked, although it falls under a rather different heading. This is healing brought about by people of mediumistic talent who claim no power in themselves but who give all the credit to the spirits of the disincarnate.

The spirits, speaking through their mediums, tell how they bring about healing. Their theories differ as widely as those of living non-medical healers, but while almost none of them appears to rely on prayer to a Higher Being, they agree that a living person of mediumistic ability is needed to work with and through. Needed also is a supply of vital force.

The fact that some mediums are thrown into a trance state strongly hints that the spirits are able to use suggestion, and, if they draw from the living enough vital force for mesmeric-hypnotic use, this accounts in part for some of the healing which is accomplished.

An excellent little book for the curious who may wish to follow this line of healing and its spirit-given explanations, is "The Mediumship of Arnold Clare", by Harry Edwards, himself a famous mediumistic healer. In it may be found described things which remind one strongly of the Huna shadowy bodies which are owned by each of the three selves, the Huna grades of vital force, the "will" power, and the thought forms charged with vital force. A spirit named "Peter", said, when asked about the healing forces, "The nearest force we know comparable to that used in producing action is magnetic force, but this force (used by spirits) is of a different quality and is stronger in character."

Psychic healing, brought about with the help of the disincarnate, is not for the average person, but we find in this healing method additional proofs that Huna theories are valid and workable.

Reduced to its simplest terms, PRAYER is, according to Huna, the calling in of the High Self to join the team of the low and middle selves so that work of a miraculous nature can be undertaken and accomplished. It is the High Self which possesses the miraculous power and the wisdom to go with it. It can see into the future in so far as coming events have been determined. It has evolved through the school of life and has accumulated all the wisdom to be gained by living for a time as a low self, and, later, as a middle self. It is the self we find at work in spirit healing where the diseased tissues of a patient are miraculously changed to healthy and normal tissues. It can give guidance and help of a marvelous nature if invited to do so.

As all who have studied Huna theories will know, the High Selves do not encroach on the privilege of free will which is the birthright of the lower selves. It must allow them to learn by experience. But, when the lower selves become aware of the fact that there is a High Self watching over them as a Guardian Angel, and come to invite it to take its full share in living, it can then guide and guard and help in endless ways. This complete integration involves the three selves, not just the lower two. It brings the good life to replace the life in which the pair of lower selves stumble along without guidance, and often bring disaster upon themselves by their conflicts and differences of beliefs, desires and dislikes.

In the books, "The Secret Science Behind Miracles" and "The Secret Science At Work", the entire question of prayer has been discussed as the central theme of Huna. While self-suggestion has been lightly touched upon in both books, it has not been until now that the full value of the use of this method as an addition to prayer has been realized and presented.

Prayer, to be effective, must be started by the middle self. It must realize some need and must decide what is to be asked of the High Self in prayer. Once the work is begun, it must cause the low self to perform its important part in making the prayer.

The low self has, as a natural talent, the ability to use telepathy. All prayer is telepathic and involves the sending of a message of thought forms over the connecting shadowy-body-substance cord to the High Self, wherever it happens to be at the time. Only the low self can send such a message. More than that, only the low self can supply the needed vital force to flow along the aka cord to the High Self and, on the flow, to carry the thought forms embodying the prayer.

The middle self needs to draw on the low self for its supply of vital force in order to change the force to the more potent thing we call "will". In a like way the High Self must be supplied with its vital force by the low self. As it observes the inviolableness of the free will of the lower selves, the High Self will draw only the slight amount of force needed for its necessary work of furnishing over-all guidance. But, when invited to direct, help and take its full part in living the triune life of its man, and when it is supplied with all the vital force necessary, it can answer prayers, the more force supplied, the swifter the answer.

We have seen how the low self is given the "seed" ideas in suggestion and how these need to be filled with the commanding force of the "will". The same thing happens in relation to the High Self when we pray, except that no suggestive force can be used to compel the High Self to react as does the low self when a set of ideas is presented. The High Self, having vastly greater wisdom and experience, has a level of free will all its own, and this is as inviolate on its level as is that of the lower selves. The High Self must be allowed to decide whether or not the thing asked for in prayer is good and wise and best in the long run. It may look into the future and see that if a certain prayer were answered, it would cause upsets and trouble later on. But if the prayer is good, and if time is given to bring the answer about as a condition or circumstance, and if the vital force is supplied and the prayer is renewed daily, the answer will eventually appear.

The average person, when confronted by an urgent need demanding prayer, cries out to God or a Higher Being with a great upsurge of emotion, asking for help. The upsurge of emotion guarantees that the low self is thoroughly impressed with the urgency of the situation. It, and it alone, creates emotions. They are a part of its hallmark, just as are memory and telepathy. Where emotion is aroused strongly, there is invariably a sudden building up of the vital force supply. This may be used in many ways. In sudden anger it is used in attacking or fighting off something or someone. In fear it is used in flight if flight is possible. And in urgent prayer, it is used automatically by the low self to make the telepathic contact with the High Self and to send the empowering flow of force with the prayer.

On the other hand, the average person, when NOT confronted with a situation of great urgency, simply does not pray. Experience of the past has usually taught the futility of such prayer. One begins to meet the situation as best one can unless desperation comes. This is a sad condition, indeed. In the High Self lies more wisdom and power than we can imagine. It is there for us to draw upon even in very small matters, for the High Self takes part fully in ALL of the life of its man, when the door is opened

94

to it and the invitation is daily extended to do so.

Ordinary prayer is child's play. It is a hit and miss repetition of set prayers, the voicing of which has too often become only a religious duty. The child who is taught the duty of reciting a prayer at bedtime may carry on the habit, once it is formed, and pray nightly, but at best, it is an amateurish performance in imitation of the very fine art of complete, effective and proper prayer.

The elements of the complete and perfect prayer are:

(1) The cooperation of all three selves.

(2) The making of the decision as to what is to be asked in prayer. This is the work of the middle self, even if guidance from the High Self is the thing which is to be asked.

(3) The making of the mental picture of the condition desired. In this task the middle self reasons from the memories furnished to it on request by the low self.

(4) The giving of the mental picture of the desired condition to the low self to present telepathically to the High Self.

(5) Here the low self takes over and begins its work behind the scenes and out of reach of the middle self. It may either obey the order to make the telepathic contact with the High Self and deliver the prayer picture, or it may pay no attention to the order. It may simply drop the mental picture of the desired condition and the memory of the order into the limbo of its vast memory storage vaults, and then go on with whatever else it may have been doing or thinking. Most prayers get no farther than this limbo. That is why self-suggestion is the incomparable tool,

over and beyond its use in bringing about the usual benefits of suggestion where prayer has no part.

With the ability to use self-suggestion, the middle self can at last go confidently about the business of making ready a prayer. Then, by using the method already described, it can charge the prayer picture with vital force to such an extent that, when the low self is relaxed, it will accept the command, together with the prayer. In both will be charges of force that will demand instant consideration and close attention. It will obey the built-in order to contact the High Self telepathically, and send to it the ideas as thought forms - together with the invaluable gift of vital force.

It is as simple as that. But it is something of inestimable value. It furnishes us with a way of getting the prayer delivered and empowered every time. It may take considerably more time to concentrate on the mental image of the desired condition to be embodied in the prayer, but the reward justifies the expenditure of endless time and effort. How else can one take thought of one's future and settle down happily to the work of making it fall along pleasant and useful paths?

Self-suggestion, therefore, is a two part process. It begins with the integration of the low and middle selves and brings the life into harmonious conditions within the limits of the two lower levels. The second part comes with the integration of the third or High Self into the team, and the laying of the broad plans for the future - plans which will take shape under intuitional guidance from the High Self, which often uses circumstances and so manipulates them that a chance happening may switch the whole

course of life from one path to another in a   most
beneficial way.

If no other satisfaction were gained, the making
of daily contact with the High Self would be a reward
sufficient in itself. Here is the deep and enduring
love which one can sense and on which one can rely
in any and all circumstances. Here is the vast wisdom of the Father half of the Utterly Trustworthy
Parental Pair. Here is the love and maternal care of
the Mother half who is one with the Father, and still
separate.

The religious injunction to pray "in my name",
has a deeper Huna meaning, but for its outward use,
one may pray to the High Self direct, and depend upon
it to send the prayer on to other and higher Entities,
even to Ultimate God, if this is necessary. If one
wishes to pray directly to God, that is permissible,
but all prayer must first go to the High Self Pair before there is any chance that it may be passed on.

A prayer to God, offered in the name of the High
Self Father-Mother Pair, fulfills all the conditions
and requirements of the Biblical injunction. We may
rely completely upon the superior wisdom and love
which works always for our good. If we do our part
to the best of our limited ability, the rest will be
done for us, exactly as it should be done.

Furthermore, the High Selves form, with others
of their stage of evolution, the Great Companies of
Shining Spirits. They are not divided and held apart
as are we who reside in physical bodies. Space and
time limit them but little. Communication is by
means of telepathy of a more advanced kind, and distance is no barrier. For this reason, groups of us
who are held apart on the lower levels are guided and

watched over by closely associated companies of High Selves - the blessed "Poe Aumakua" of the kahunas.

If one should wish to make many wonderful and powerful friends in the highest places, the Great Company is the place to begin. And how does one go about contacting and attracting the helpful love and friendship of those in such high places?

Simply help those on this level of life who need help, and the gratitude of their High Selves - who are often cut off and are unable to help their stumbling charges - will be as an enduring light on one's path. These friends of the Great Company may be asked, through your own High Self, to help you help those over whom they brood as Guardian Angels. And they will help mightily. If one wishes to receive life's most radiant and enduring gifts, the way leads to and through SERVICE.

If one serves faithfully and demonstrates trustworthiness with what is given of material things or of wisdom - if one uses the increasing gifts to help others on the physical or mental side of life - there will never be a lack of means with which to serve.

Of all human satisfactions, there is none greater than that of being able to serve and to love. And loving and selfless service is the shortest and most direct road leading to evolutionary growth and progress. It is the road leading to growth from the level of the middle self to that of the High Self. It is the Royal Road. It is a very high and exclusive road guarded against intrusion by all the barriers of ignorance, selfishness and hate. But even the most humble of us can enter it freely if we make our first hesitant step one into Service-With-Love. Once this step is purposefully taken with eyes fastened on the

98

shining goal of progression, it will be discovered that there is no need to wait for a distant day of reward. The reward is waiting on the road at the end of each smallest step, and it is called by the sages who have passed that way, "The Joy of Service," than which there is none greater - none more enduring.

APPENDIX

In past ages, several arts, sciences and other unclassified but compact units of knowledge were developed by slow steps to various levels of perfection.

The science of Mathematics was sufficiently exact to allow almost full perfection. The several arts which were developed have not been greatly advanced even in modern times, although such things as Law, Medicine, Physics and Sociology have advanced to new levels.

Of the unclassified but compact units of knowledge, only one was pushed almost to the top level. This was the unit which we are coming to call "Huna" or, to give the word its translation, "The Secret".

Huna is difficult to classify because it includes at least three poorly developed sciences, two of them still in their infancy, Psychology and Psychic Science. These are the sciences of man considered as a conscious being who lives in a physical body during the period of earthly life, but survives and lives in a different "body" after death. A branch of Psychology which also needs to be included in any survey, is that now studied as a condition of consciousness in which the vague thing called "mind" functions improperly. This is still labeled Abnormal Psychology. It deals with such things as dual personality changes.

Belonging to this classification also is Religion. It is farthest of all from reaching scientific standing.

In sorry fact, it becomes more and more darkened and muddled year by year as dogmas and cults increase, almost all based on "revelation" instead of the sciences of consciousness.

Religion is, in reality, the science of the relationship between man and any living beings higher or more evolved than himself who may have an influence on his life, either here or hereafter.

Ethics or Morals should be considered as separate departments, and naturally fall under Sociology, although always mingling with Religion.

The science of Huna can and does cover and include all of the items listed above. This would make it so complicated that a mountain of books could not describe it fully were it not for the fact that all the dogmas, misinformation and speculations which now clutter or block the paths of the several branches of the one actual science are absent in the approach to Huna.

The known and deduced history of Huna is a very fascinating chapter which carries us from the most remote times up to the present moment.

Little is actually known of the origin of Huna. It may be deduced, however, from the fact that part of the lore can be recognized in the earliest recorded writings of Egypt, that the priests or "Keepers of the Secret" (kahunas), had either lived in the land of the Nile or had been in contact for some time with its peoples.

As Huna possessed a simple version of its secret science as well as a more complicated and carefully guarded version for the more intelligent, we find in early Egypt the simple or exoteric part of the knowledge presented openly and in such a form that

101

even the men of low intelligence could grasp and use some of the values.

The esoteric or initiatory material of Huna was kept within the hereditary priesthood of the kahunas, never being written down. But in order to allow a lasting and foolproof account of Huna to be preserved for all the ages, a special language was invented, providing a means of giving an inner and outer meaning to any statement of the teachings. Such statements as were made in this "sacred language" formed a code which could not be broken unless one already was familiar with at least part of the Huna lore and with the word-symbols used to name elements of the system.

It is evident that the kahunas and their people made up a race apart from the Egyptians and others with whom they either lived or were closely associated. It is also rather clear that, sometime between the Mosaic and Christian periods, they left and began a long migration to find new homes in what we now call "Polynesia". In their new homes, speaking only the "sacred language", they flourished for a number of centuries, preserving intact their language and the secret knowledge which it had been constructed to conceal and yet reveal.

In their new Pacific Island homes, the kahunas used no writing, depending on memory alone to keep Huna pure and intact. But the initiate kahunas who remained behind, and who may have been of a different race, allowed the writing down of teachings from Huna. The writing was never done in any dialect of the "sacred language", but original statements were translated invariably into some other tongue. This hid from the eyes of the curious the words which had originally been made to carry double meanings, and made it all but impossible for anyone not familiar with the language of the "Secret" to break the code.

The initiates remaining in the Near East after the migration of the ancestors of the Polynesians, took it upon themselves to put much of Huna into the veiled forms of writing. They produced the Gnostic writings as well as much which was later incorporated with other materials in assembling the New Testament. Some of the veiled writings also crept into later parts of the Old Testament which already contained much Huna legendary lore, of which the story of the Creation and of the Garden of Eden may be said to be typical.

In late years a long study was conducted in Polynesia which resulted, in the year 1931, in the discovery that there had been such a secret system as that of Huna, and in the partial breaking of the code so that the inner teachings could be laid bare. However, it was not until about the year 1950 that the coded Huna contained in the Gnostic and New Testament writings were recognized. At that time it was seen that by translating these writings back into one of the Polynesian dialects, preferably the Hawaiian, the inner teachings could be brought to light through the use of the ancient code.

The inner or esoteric teachings of the Gnostic and Christian writings were found to be that part of Huna always retained for the initiates. The parables attributed to Jesus furnished excellent examples of the way the code was used from times immemorial. The simple outer meaning intended for the less intelligent masses lies on the surface, teaching some simple lesson, but hidden by the code is to be found information running parallel with all the best findings of modern Psychology and Psychic Science, that is, in so far as they have limped ahead. In addition, the rediscovered Huna system adds much more information to what we have managed to evolve for ourselves before arriving at the present stalemate in those lines of research.

Huna corroborates all we know of the subconscious and conscious parts of mind, but adds much invaluable information about their natures, forces and special abilities. It presents to us the superconscious and shows its characteristics in turn. As to man in his abnormal mental states, Huna offers some enlightenment where simple disease is not at fault. But, when it comes to the explanation of the startling things uncovered by Psychic Science in its studies of spirits and the "supernatural", Huna offers the only explanations ever found which will explain the mechanics of everything from telepathy to table tipping: from prediction and psychometry to the temporary return in the flesh of the "materialized" dead.

Any person who may wish to check on Huna findings can now purchase a good Hawaiian-English dictionary and a Hawaiian-English New Testament to use in examining the surprisingly clever way in which the original kahunas placed double meanings in words and roots of compounded words to conceal the inner meanings while laying open the outer. The language is very simple to work with in this way, and with the addition of the knowledge of the meaning of a few symbol word meanings, checking can proceed with ease. The main symbol words are "light", for the High Self; "water" for any of the three grades of vital force used by the three "selves" of the man, and "heavy breathing" for the accumulation of extra vital force to be used by the low self in various activities which fall under the heading of "psychic", these including telepathy, the use of mesmerism or any form of suggestion, prayer made in the Huna manner to the High Self, and the production of spiritistic phenomena by the disincarnate including table tipping, levitation, poltergeist activities and even full materialization, apports and transportation. Any mention of the symbol words for "cords, threads, tubes, water ditches or ropes" will point to the sending of a flow of vital force through a strand of invisible or "shadowy" (ectoplasmic) material which may connect the low self with another person or, especially, with its own High Self. The "knot" indicates any of the several things which may prevent such a flow of vital force from the low self to the High Self. A similar symbol meaning is found in any reference to a block or other obstruction of a path. In the Bible, from Isaiah through the New Testament, the "stumbling block" in the path is the symbol most often used, but the "cross" and "crown of thorns" also symbolize these "knots" which we think of as "fixations, complexes or spirit obsessions".

Considering the ease with which anyone can run a check on the present Huna findings, even with no knowledge at all of the Hawaiian language, there is really no excuse at all for anyone to refuse to consider the proofs and evidences which are so greatly important to the sciences covered by Huna in its very wide scope, or the new and penetrating light which it throws on Religion, especially Christianity and those religions in which early Yoga forms a part.

Admittedly, it is and will continue to be hard for

those who have accepted the religious beliefs of any branch of Christianity to bring themselves to face the possibility that what they have come to believe as all the truth possible to obtain, is only the outer part of a large whole. Those who believe that they have already taken all needed steps to win "salvation", may be distressed to learn that there are "mystery" teachings which need to be understood before the full "salvation" can be attained.

While some mention of the inner teachings have remained in the accepted New Testament, much has either been lost or edited out, although many passages containing Huna symbol words have remained, such as, in John I: 10-12:

"The same came for a witness, to bear witness of the Light (High Self symbol), that all men might through him believe.

"He was not that Light, but was sent to bear witness of that Light.

"That was the true Light, which lighteth every man that cometh into the world."

Two of the early Church Fathers, Clement and Origen, writing in the years around 200 A.D., gave complete evidence of the existence of the inner side of the Christian teachings. For an easy checking source of this material, Annie Besant's book, "Esoteric Christianity", is recommended. It is to be found in most libraries as it has been placed there by the Theosophical Society. Here are some passages quoted by Mrs. Besant:

Clement, in his "Miscellanies":

"The Lord...allowed us to communicate of those divine Mysteries, and of that holy light, to those who are able to receive them. They did not certainly disclose to the many what did not belong to the many; but to the few to whom He knew that they belonged, who were capable of receiving and being moulded according to them. But secret things are entrusted to speech, not to writing, as is the case with God. And if one say that it is written, 'There is nothing secret which shall not be revealed, nor hidden which shall not be disclosed, 'let him also hear from us, that to him who hears secretly, even what is secret shall be manifested. . . . . And to him who is able secretly to observe what is delivered to him, that which is veiled shall be disclosed as truth; and what is hidden to many shall appear manifest to the few. . . . The Mysteries are delivered mystically, that what is spoken may be in the mouth of the speaker; rather not in his voice, but in his understanding. . . . . "

Note the effort made in this passage to explain and still not explain fully, the fact that a foreign set of words had to be used, and when spoken, must be understood by the one to be initiated. For instance, if the word "water" was used in explaining some part of the Mysteries to the candidate, it would be meaningless unless its hidden meaning of "vital force" had been divulged. It is probable that the necessity for using the words from the "sacred language", caused the eventual loss of the knowledge of the Mysteries. To memorize and retain the symbol words without first learning to speak the complete language, would be difficult. Substituting of words would soon result in the loss or changing of original meanings. In India it is to be supposed that the early writers on Yoga were at least partly initiated into Huna, for the basic Huna method of accumulating extra "mana", or vital force, for various uses was slowly developed into a set of elaborate breathing exercises, while the Sanskrit word, "prana", which means "breath" or "to breathe", came into use to replace the Huna word, "mana". Or it is possible that some effort to give the symbol or code meaning of Huna, in which "to breathe hard" ("ha") stood for the accumulation and use of vital force.

To return to the evidence of the existence of the inner teaching in Christianity, let us consider statements made by Origen:

"The object of Christianity is that we should become wise. If you come to the books written after the time of Jesus, you will find that those multitudes of believers who hear the parables are, as it were, 'without', and worthy only of exoteric doctrines, while the disciples learn in private the explanation of the parables. For, privately, to his own disciples did Jesus open up all things, esteeming above the multitudes those who desired to know His wisdom. "

Here is another bit from Origen which explains how the inner teachings were worked as symbols into supposed historical records. "It is sufficient, however, to represent in the style of a historic narrative what is intended to convey a secret meaning in the garb of history, that those who have the capacity may work out for themselves all that relates to the subject.....Now, in the next place, if any one has the capacity let him understand that in what assumes the form of history, and which contains some things that are literally true, while yet it conveys a deeper meaning.......these remarks are to be understood as being made by us with a concealed meaning.... "

In the Gnostic writings, of course, may be found a large variety of attempts to record the substance of

Huna or similar mystery teachings without revealing too much. Whether or not the kahunas originated the system of presenting inner and outer teachings, it is not to be denied that in the early Egyptian times when Huna ideas were being absorbed and distorted in the process, there was the secret knowledge reserved for the initiates and mentioned in the inner temple. A similar tradition existed among the Jews where the "veil" of the sanctuary symbolized the division into inner and outer teachings.

In giving an outline of the ten simple elements of which Huna is composed, it can be shown how very simple the system was and is. However, because these elements name things often completely unfamiliar to the reader, or because they name something similar to items about which the reader already has set opinions, there needs to be much explaining and a very considerable effort to show why the Huna concepts are more reasonable than those held in the several modern schools of thought. These expanded presentations may be found in earlier books on Huna, especially "The Secret Science Behind Miracles".

In Huna man is said to be made up of nine parts which are possessed both in life and in the condition of survival after death. One more part, the human physical body raises the count of parts to ten during life on this level.

Primarily, man is made up of three "selves" or spirits. These count as three parts of the man.

Each "self" or spirit of the triune man has a thin and invisible body in which to live. These count as three more parts. They are the "bodies" in which the "selves" live if separated by any chance during physical life or after death. Normally the low and middle selves blend and intermix their "Shadowy" bodies and surround and impregnate the physical body with them during life, but withdraw and live on together after death as disincarnate spirits. The High Self always lives apart in its own "Shadowy" or "aka" body, to use the Hawaiian word.

Each self possesses the life force or vital force, which is called "mana" by the kahunas, and which is symbolized as "water". There are three grades or potencies of this life force, and each is counted as a part of the man, adding up to a total of nine.

The physical body counts as one part, when it is being used, and so the number 10 has come down to us as the "perfect number".

The number 3 is a symbol standing for either the three selves, the three shadowy bodies or the three grades of mana or vital force.

The number 4 symbolizes the low self, its vital force, its shadowy body and the physical body, over which it has charge.

All such uses of numbers and geometric figures such as that of the triangle, the five pointed star and the cross, have been used in the past, and one who knows the significance of the symbols knows Huna in broad outline. To know how to use the knowledge of the ten elements is, of course, less simple.

We have seen that in the use of mesmerism and suggestion, there are involved elements not included in the list of human elements but similar in some ways to one of them. For instance, we have the tiny thought forms which are made by actions of the consciousness of the two lower selves. These are given bodies made of the shadowy substance of the low self, and they can float along on a flow of vital force as it moves by way of a shadowy thread or cord from one person to another, producing a telepathic response. Or the thought forms may flow with the gift of empowering vital force to the High Self as the "seed" from which the answer to the prayer will be grown to maturity and made manifest on the physical level.

The unrationalized thoughts or impressions held by the low self form the fixations or complexes which are so important to Huna and are symbolized by the cross of the crucifixion (or the simple X cross denoting that a path is closed), as well as the "stumbling block in the path". Here again we have thought forms in bodies made of the invisible ectoplasmic substance.

A companion piece to the complex is the disincarnate spirit, be it a low or a middle self, of the sort referred to as "devils" in the New Testament. These dead individuals may be made up of a low plus a middle self, in which case thay are normal spirits. Or the two selves may have been separated by some accident of death or because of long illness and unconscious periods prior to death. In any event, the low self alone (being irrational and so more dangerous) or the normal two-self spirit may obsess the living to some degree. Complete obsession means insanity, but partial obsession may show as a large or small degree of response to the control exerted on the living by the obsessive dead. While such influencing of the living by the dead is usually bad, it can be for good, although the spirits moved by a desire to bring good are seldom long in contact with the physical level of life after their passing over.

A further addition to the ten elements of man, as

found in Huna, relates to spirits or entities ranging higher or falling lower than man in the evolutionary march. Above the High Selves are said to be level after level of Higher Beings, some once having been humans, some not. Below the human level range the lesser entities, most of whom are evolving slowly upward toward life as men. However, there is ever provided a body made of the shadowy substance in some degree or other of rarification for the entity to inhabit, and there is always some potency of the life force or "mana".

The Huna lore presents no perfected God, but, instead, a great and ever-evolving conglomerate of consciousness evolving from low to high, and always embodied in some form of the shadowy substance while empowered or made alive by the life force in some of its many potencies or vibrational rates.

Each evolutionary level of life is marked by its characteristic awareness as a level of conscious being. The low self has only the reasoning ability of the higher animals, itself still being an animal in a body. But it has the power of memory.

The middle self does not remember. It relies on the low self to do all the remembering for the man while it uses inductive reason, which is its mental gift, and so is able to guide the low self.

The High Self has a still more evolved type of mentation which is difficult for the lower selves to understand except to see what such mentation can accomplish in action. It can see into the future to a certain distance and can change the future to a large extent for the individual if asked to do so and if given a steady daily supply of the basic vital force to use in making the changes. It can use the vital force to make instant changes in physical matter under the right conditions, and so bring about instant healing. The limits of its ability to make such miraculous changes remains unknown in so far as that part of Huna which has been recovered to date is concerned.

The departments of Ethics or Morals, in Huna, are covered by the negative command NOT to hurt others, and on the positive side of the inner teaching by the command to love and help where this is possible. One is the command for the animal or low self and for the less evolved masses. The other is for the more evolved and intelligent as represented by the middle self, and exemplified in the lives of the High Selves and Higher Beings of all levels.

ADDENDUM

The full exploration of the possibilities of working with the High Self, once contact is made through the use of self-suggestion, has not been completed.

At this time we cannot say what miracles can be performed with the help of the High Self, but, looking back at the instant healing accomplished by the kahunas of yesterday, we are encouraged to expect great and wonderful things.

In India, where self-suggestion after the Huna manner has been practiced for centuries by the devotees of Yoga, the belief that one must suffer in order to repay karmic indebtedness has prevented the use of healing potentials.

To list the possibilities, once full working contact is established between the three selves, we may safely put down:

1. Miraculous healing, both instant and slow.
2. Seeing to a limited extent into the future.
3. Obtaining High Self guidance and help.

Here in the Western world, where we are in our first approach to this part of the field, we are, however, not without instances of partial development of the abilities in question.

On pages 316-317 of "The Secret Science Behind Miracles" may be found the story of one of the first American mesmerists, Phineas Quimby, and an account of how, under mesmeric control, his favorite subject, Lucius, was accidentally found to be able to exhibit supernormal abilities. He could see what was going on at a distance, and could diagnose physical ills and heal them. Quimby had long suffered from kidney trouble and was healed by the laying on of a

114

hand by Lucius while under mesmeric influence but suddenly seeming to act of his own volition. This healing was instantaneous, and it lasted. That it was accomplished by something wiser and more able than the normal Lucius was evident to the mind of Quimby, and, while he had no knowledge of Huna, of course, he attributed the strange powers to some Consciousness higher than man and lower than Ultimate God. He called it the "Wisdom" or the "Power".

It makes no difference whether this contact with the High Self "Wisdom-Power" was made through the use of mesmerism or not. Hypnotic suggestion or self-suggestion would have accomplished the same results.

A more modern and well documented case which falls under the same classification is that of the late Edgar Cayce. In a trance condition usually induced by hypnotic suggestion administered by an associate, he exhibited abilities not possessed in his normal state. While this ability did not include such instant and direct healing as that exhibited by Quimby's subject, Lucius, it included similar prescriptions of remedies and the same diagnostic procedure.

Judging from the records of Quimby, the full contact with the "Wisdom" was rare on the part of Lucius, and many times a diagnosis and prescription proved to be useless. On the other hand, if Cayce failed to make a correct diagnosis or to describe the right remedy, little is said of it in the books which tell of his life and work.

Cayce frequently found obscure causes of illness or pain. In one instance he diagnosed the illness of a young man as something caused by a cracked vertebra in his neck. He then stated that a special form of operation was needed to correct the trouble, and that there was only one doctor skilled in this technique. Asked who this doctor might be and where he was to be found, he gave his name and Boston address, adding that at the moment he was in Europe, but that on a certain date he would return. This information was found later to be correct from first to last. The doctor operated and the young man recovered. Many such cases were recorded, and the transcribed records are still in process of being studied and classified by an organization headed by his son, Hugh, formed to carry on this work.

It is interesting to note that Cayce advanced no set theory to explain his work. He knew that he made contact in trance conditions with some source of information far wiser and more able than himself. On one point he stood firm. This was in his denial that his work was in any way based on the aid of the disembodied or spirit dead. He recognized no "guide" or helper such as Spiritualistic mediums so often mention in their psychic work. (In passing, it must be said that many such spirit helpers have correctly diagnosed, prescribed and healed directly, even instantly, but their number is painfully small, and the pretenders to power are legion on the spirit levels.)

In the early years of Cayce's healing efforts the subject of reincarnation was not mentioned, but, after he fell in with a gentleman who believed in the Theosophical version of reincarnation, he began to peer back into the past lives of his patients, often stating that certain troubles were caused by one or more events in past lives. He described these lives at times in some detail.

Since the work of Edgar Cayce has become widely known (through books like Segrue's "There Is A River", and the excellent books on the reincarnation angles by Miss Gina Cerminara, as well as through publications issued by The Association for Research and Enlightenment, headed by Mr. Hugh Cayce) there have appeared individuals endeavoring to make "life readings" similar to those made by Edgar Cayce. Usually, because of new and stringent laws against psychic diagnosis and the prescription of remedies, the work is confined to readings of past lives, and, because such readings can seldom be checked, their accuracy is open to question.

The use of hypnotic suggestion is also coming rapidly under restrictive laws, so, in the future it is probable that any person interested (as many are) in trying their hands at contact and direct work with the High Selves will have to use self-suggestion to reach the state needed for contact and work. Given time and success on the part of those who experiment, the medical world may eventually find in this corner of the field things of great value which merit attention and use.

Perhaps the only precaution to be taken in testing out the use of self-suggestion to try to duplicate the work of men like Cayce, is to make doubly sure that contact is not made with the spirit of a dead man, but with one's own High Self. Many spirits have, in the past, been contacted, and a few have claimed to be the High Self of the experimenter, but when they failed to show superior wisdom or power, they were seen to be what they actually were, lying pretenders. A great Huna initiate living in Judea long ago gave sage advice when he once said, "By their fruits ye shall know them."

BOOKS ON HUNA
By MAX FREEDOM LONG

THE SECRET SCIENCE BEHIND MIRACLES. The basic book of the series. It reveals how the *kahunas* of Hawaii were able to perform authentic miracles of healing, change bad situations for their clients, see into the future and do many incredible things—all because they knew and used an ancient and highly perfected system of psychological knowledge called *Huna,* meaning "The Secret." This secret lore is fully described. It includes all that is known in modern Psychology and Psychical Research, but goes far beyond these to add knowledge at which we have hardly guessed.

THE SECRET SCIENCE AT WORK. This book tells of the work of the HUNA RESEARCH ASSOCIATES to prove the validity of the *Huna* principles and the practicality of using them today. Much added information is given on allied lines, including the language-code proof that the ancient system was the inner, secret teaching in parts of the Bible, especially in passages in the New Testament, and also in related Gnostic writings.

GROWING INTO LIGHT. Here are simplified instructions to help the individual, working alone, to use *Huna* in his own life.

SELF-SUGGESTION and the New Huna Theory of Mesmerism and Hypnosis. Here is another striking example of how *Huna* more than doubles modern psychological knowledge. At last we have a theory which fully covers this field. This book has become a text for amateur and professional alike, but is primarily aimed at teaching the layman to use the very helpful method of self-suggestion.

PSYCHOMETRIC ANALYSIS. *Huna* is again the basis of an explanation of psychic abilities, in this case of psychometry. ESP at last is put to practical use. Psychic impressions of which one is unaware can be amplified and sensed. This reconstructed form of "biometric" testing makes possible a new and better way to determine the I.Q. and good or bad character.

THE HUNA CODE IN RELIGIONS. What Jesus taught in secret to his Disciples, and what Buddha taught to his selected followers.

The HUNA CODE In RELIGIONS

Readers of Mr. Long's book, **The Secret Science Behind Miracles,** know how he uncovered the secrets which enabled the **Kahunas** of Hawaii to perform miracles for their people. The secret lay in the understanding of man's mental and spiritual powers and how to **use** them. Mr. Long, after years of study, **broke a CODE built upon the multiple meanings of words used by the Kahunas.**

After the Code became more fully understood, Mr. Long and his Huna Research Associates made a surprising discovery. They found that **the same Code had been used to graft onto many passages in the New Testament the inner teachings of Huna.** This discovery was reported and a brief preliminary outline of the findings given in the book, **The Secret Science at Work. But the surface had only been scratched.**

Research continued slowly, with many more Code meanings being uncovered, and more and more of the hidden teachings of coded sacred writings brought to life. **An entirely new insight into the nature and work of Jesus resulted as the things which he taught in secret to the Disciples were decoded.**

The extra-canonical books which had not been given a place in the New Testament soon came under similar investigations, and eventually included the Old Testament, Gnostic and Mystery writing, with the trail leading on to **the basic secrets of Yoga and esoteric Buddhism.** The use of the Code slowly expanded the finding of the original work done on Hawaiian Kahunas. The four Gospels became a mine of information which was so strange and unexpected that **a burst of new light began to illuminate teachings which had been incomplete for centuries.**

REINCARNATION, which had been lost to Christianity and drawn out to endlessness by the priests of India, was restored to its rational form in both systems of belief.

The **SALVATION** of Christianity and the **escape into Nirvana** of Buddhism, came in for the most extensive revision through the Code. The Apostle, Paul, was seen NOT to have been an initiate into the Huna lore, as were the Disciples. His assertion that Jesus had to die on the cross to SAVE mankind from the curse of Adamic sin, was found to be the poor guess of an outsider. BUT there were TWO TRUE SALVATIONS which the **inner teachings** of Jesus (to say nothing of Buddha), made known, and now that they **are known,** men can begin to work out their Salvation by TWO graduated steps. The first step is to be taken during life, and the second consummated after death—its magnificent reward being the condition hidden under the Code-symbol of "The Kingdom of Heaven," and "Nirvana".

From **YOGA,** the Code has extracted a method whose meaning has long been lost. This method is the very heart of the **"Prayer of the Miracle"** which Jesus taught the Disciples to use.

A DICTIONARY of the CODE words (as well as a full list of word-symbols) has been included in this new book. So there can be no question of validity, the words and their multiple meanings are photographed from the invaluable Hawaiian-English Dictionary printed a century ago. It enables the reader to check Mr. Long's findings and perhaps make more discoveries.